VISIONS
of
HEAVEN

ALSO BY

Jane Moe

What Heaven Is Like

VISIONS

of

HEAVEN

WHAT MY
NEAR-DEATH
EXPERIENCE
Taught Me
ABOUT ETERNITY

WRITTEN BY
JANE MOE
WITH
SUZY BILLS

CFI
An imprint of Cedar Fort, Inc.
Springville, Utah

ISBN 13: 978-1-4621-2191-5

Published by CFI, an imprint of Cedar Fort, Inc.
2373 W. 700 S., Springville, UT 84663
Distributed by Cedar Fort, Inc., www.cedarfort.com

LIBRARY OF CONGRESS CATALOGING-IN-PUBLICATION DATA

Names: Moe, Jane, 1953- author. | Bills, Suzy, 1981- author.
Title: Visions of heaven : what my near-death experience taught me about eternity / Jane Moe and Suzy Bills.
Description: Springville, Utah : CFI, an imprint of Cedar Fort, Inc., [2018] | Includes bibliographical references and index.
Identifiers: LCCN 2018004028 (print) | LCCN 2018007071 (ebook) | ISBN 9781462128877 (epub, pdf, mobi) | ISBN 9781462121915 (perfect bound : alk. paper)
Subjects: LCSH: Moe, Jane, 1953- | Near-death experiences--Religious aspects--Church of Jesus Christ of Latter-day Saints. | Near-death experiences--Religious aspects--Mormon Church.
Classification: LCC BX8643.F87 (ebook) | LCC BX8643.F87 M64 2018 (print) | DDC 289.3092/2--dc23
LC record available at https://lccn.loc.gov/2018004028

Cover design by Shawnda T. Craig
Cover design © 2018 Cedar Fort, Inc.
Edited and typeset by Kathryn Watkins and Kaitlin Barwick

Printed in the United States of America

10 9 8 7 6 5 4 3 2 1

Printed on acid-free paper

This book is dedicated to my eternal husband, Richard Powers Moe.
You have always believed in me, and this twelve-year journey to
release this book would not have happened if it wasn't for you.

This is OUR story, not just mine.
I adore you.

Jane

Contents

Prologue

THE JOURNEY BEGINS

As I wake up from the anesthesia, I see Richard next to me. He kneels beside the gurney and tenderly takes my hand. I slur out, "I saw your dad while they were operating on me."

Richard shakes his head as if to clear it, thinking he's heard me wrong. "Honey, what did you say?" Leaning closer, he whispers in my ear, "Sweetheart, my dad is dead, remember?"

I smile as I continue speaking. "I saw heaven, and your daddy was there. He said that he goes by Junior or Kim but that his real name is Kilmer Oscar Jr. He told me he was born in the Philippines and then grew up in Hawaii. And he hated wearing shoes. When he did wear shoes, he wouldn't tie the laces."

Richard's jaw drops, and I can feel his hands trembling. He's not shocked that I believe I've seen heaven but that I know details about his father. Richard was just fifteen when his father died, and the death was so painful for Richard that he's never told me anything about his father aside from his unexpected death.

I ramble on about my visit with Junior, the radiating light, and the immense feeling of God's love. A nurse comes by to adjust an IV bottle, and I excitedly point at her. "You have angels on your shoulders!"

The nurse smiles at Richard. "We hear things like that all the time after patients come out of surgery."

Richard is sure the staff hear some strange things all right, but this? How is it possible? He turns to me, hungry for more information about his dad.

"Richard, your dad is terrific. He told me not to be afraid, that I would survive the surgery because it's not my time yet." Closing my eyes, I retell the rest of my beautiful vision. "Junior wanted me to feel God's love. As he placed his hand on the golden door, he said, 'I'll open it just a little—no more. You're not ready yet to understand everything heaven has to offer.'"

Richard looks at the nurse again, questions evident in his eyes. The nurse simply smiles and shrugs her shoulders.

Retelling the dream to Richard is exhausting, and I'm starting to fall asleep. As I give in, letting my eyelids close, Richard kisses my forehead and tells me, "I love you, honey. I'll be here when you wake up."

As the pain medication takes over, I'm able to mumble one final thought. "The last thing I remember Junior saying was, 'Please, Jane, tell Richard to do as I've done and never let go. Tell him families can be forever.'"

At the time, I didn't realize the full meaning of Junior's words, but I knew a father had reached down from heaven to touch his son. This was the start of a grand journey—a journey that still continues—one in which I've learned that the Father of us all reaches down from heaven to let us know He loves us. Along the way, I've learned about God's true gospel and the opportunity to one day live with our families in heaven.

Chapter 1

A Prayer That Opened the Heavens

The days leading up to the surgery and dream had been stressful. While walking down the street in Hollywood Hills, I had slipped on a wet manhole cover and came crashing to the ground. Every bone in my left ankle had shattered. The ER physicians told me I would need surgery to (hopefully) repair the damage. They gave me a list of orthopedic surgeons, and I began calling them and making appointments. One by one, each surgeon examined the x-rays of my ankle and then shook his head, telling me the damage couldn't be repaired. I was devastated—and in a lot of pain.

I had already given up hope when Richard convinced me to visit one more specialist. Richard guided my wheelchair into the doctor's office, and I waited in agony, already knowing what the clinician would tell me.

After Dr. Burns looked at the x-rays, he turned to me. "I think we can put you back together again." I felt a glimmer of hope. But then he added, "It will be an exceptionally long surgery, and it could take a long time to recover. But with hard work on your part, I think you'll be able to walk again."

I took a long, deep breath and then began to cry. "Why did this happen to me?" I wailed.

As Richard wheeled me out to the car and carefully helped me get somewhat comfortable in the back seat, I felt angry, sad, and depressed. As I continued to cry, I asked, "Why, God? Why?" As I lay there wallowing in self-pity, I had no idea that God would soon be blessing me beyond what I could have imagined. In His infinite wisdom, He was allowing me to face a harrowing trial so that I would be ready to seek His help and receive a message from Him.

Though I dreaded the surgery, at least I didn't have to wait long for it—it was scheduled for two days after the initial visit with Dr. Burns. The night before, intense fear was fighting with the physical pain I was experiencing.

Richard tried to calm me. "Honey, Dr. Burns does this kind of operation every day. After it's over, you can finally heal."

I was in such agony that I retorted, "Richard, your own father was in the hospital for what should have been a routine procedure, and he ended up dying." I immediately regretted my words. "I'm so sorry," I sobbed, "but I'm afraid. Afraid I'll leave you just like your dad did."

It was later that night that I gingerly got to my knees and began praying to God, and then to Richard's father. Though I had faith in prayer, I never imagined that Richard's father would not only hear my prayers but also visit me because of my plea for help.

I see myself lying, unconscious, on the surgery table, surrounded by medical staff. How is this possible? If I'm down there, how can I also be looking at myself from above? Immediately the confusion is replaced by another sensation as I'm engulfed in a bright light that caresses and soothes me. Though I'm astonished, I'm not afraid. The light begins to part, and I notice a swirl of gleaming gold clouds. My body and my soul are engulfed in a love so intense that I begin to weep tears of joy.

Wiping my face, I see a door in front of me. It's slightly ajar, with a brilliant light bursting from the opening. I've never seen anything brighter, more magnificent, and I feel compelled to draw nearer, to see what's on the other side of the door. I know that whatever it is, it's good. Actually, much better than *good*.

I know I must be in heaven.

The door, gleaming the hue of pure gold, had been opened by the man standing in front of me, who is radiating the same intense light that's spilling from behind the door. I don't recognize him, but he has an aura of indescribable beauty, of youth and health. Perfection, even. The robe he's wearing ends just above his feet, and at first I think he has wings, but then I realize it's just more of his billowing garment. Around him, I can actually *see* waves of joy, peace, and knowledge.

My eyes widen as a new thought comes to me. If this is heaven, then is he . . .

"Are you God?"

"No, but He sent me to visit you." The man has a gentle, lyrical voice that fills me with warmth. Then he adds, "Jane, we heard you when you were praying last night."

I had been praying because I was scared about the ankle surgery that would take place in the morning—the surgery I had apparently died from if I was now in heaven. While praying, I had pleaded earnestly that God would keep me safe, especially since the love of my life, Richard, had lost his father during a routine medical procedure. I was afraid I would die too, breaking Richard's heart again. As I continued to pray, I started talking with Richard's dad, telling him how sorry I was that he'd died when Richard was a teenager, how I wished I could have known the man Richard admired so deeply. I'd also asked Richard's dad to pray for me, that I wouldn't die like he had. I figured since he was already in heaven, maybe his prayers had more sway with the powers that be.

Turning my thoughts back to the present, I wonder, *If the man in front of me isn't God but he heard my prayers, who is he?* Before I can verbalize the question, he answers it.

"I'm Junior, Richard's dad. You're with me in the spirit world." He pauses. Then, with great reverence in his voice, he asks, "May I share something incredible with you?"

Perhaps I should be frightened, but instead I feel peaceful. Somehow I know this glorious being is indeed Richard's father, and it seems like he already knows me. I can see it in his shining eyes, which have a depth I've never seen before. I trust him completely.

I nod my head, and he continues to speak: "I want you to feel how much God loves you." And that's when he opens the door, just a quarter of an inch. I gasp as I realize that light isn't the only thing pouring out. Coming through even more abundantly is God's love. The love is so intense that I'm overwhelmed. It races through my body like electricity and at the same time fills me so fully that I think I'll burst. I've never before felt so much love. Or such perfect love—somehow I know that's what it is. This perfect love is as pure, white, and radiant as the light that engulfs Richard's dad.

Through the narrow opening I can see angels surrounding Jesus, more brilliant than anything I've ever seen before. Again, I feel waves and more waves of His love crash over me. Now, rather than being overwhelming, it's invigorating. Jesus's love is evident in His eyes—the type of eyes that can see into the soul. Though He can see all my imperfections, there's no judgment, only love.

Everything else is stunning too. The colors are more vibrant than any on earth. Red is not simply red. It is brilliant and shimmery, appearing to have gold flecks in it. The same is true of the blues, greens, and every other color I see as my eyes dart back and forth, taking in this magnificent scene. The hues are so vivid that they seem to be alive. I also hear music. Each note is profound, strong yet whispering. Its soothing ebbs and flows swirl around me and through me.

I reach toward the sound and light, yearning to see more and to be enveloped more fully in God's love. "How beautiful," I exclaim. Then, turning to Junior, I tell him, "I want to come with you! I want to be in heaven!" I'm sure he can hear the pleading in my voice.

"No," he says, gently shaking his head. "I'm sorry, but you must stay. Jane, please take care of my son for me."

Looking into Junior's kind eyes and seeing his beaming smile, I know he's right. I need to stay on earth so I can be with Richard. Though the thought of leaving the glorious light and engulfing love of God is almost physically painful, I nod my head to let Junior know I understand.

Though my first journey into heaven has been brief, I've learned much. And I will never be afraid of death again.

As Richard drove me home from the hospital after the surgery, I kept thinking about the divine light and love that had encompassed me when I'd seen heaven. I wanted to return and to speak with Richard's father again. But how could I? Junior had told me it wasn't my time to die, so how could I return to heaven and see him again? I continued to ponder this question as Richard carried me inside our house and tucked me into bed. Soon I was drifting to sleep.

As I sleep, I hear a voice—a new one. "Hi, Jane. I'm Richard's grandfather, Kilmer Oscar Sr."

My brain tells me I'm sleeping, so the voice doesn't faze me. But then I hear it again, and this time I see the person who's speaking. Peering intently at me is an attractive man with caring eyes. He has his arm around his son, Junior. "You remember my son, of course—Richard's dad." Both men, radiating light, smile as they see the look of recognition—mixed with astonishment—on my face.

I grin back. "Yes, I wanted to enter heaven with you!"

Junior is beaming, pleased that I haven't forgotten him. He reaches into the beautiful glow around him and takes the hand of a woman. As she steps out of the light and into full view, I can see that she's beautiful. "This is Richard's mother, Marjorie Jane," Junior explains.

She reaches out to me and cups my face in her hands. After kissing me on both cheeks, she says, "Dear, sweet Jane, I've waited so long for this moment! We're excited to be here with you." As she slips an arm around my waist, she continues: "We've been trying to reach you and our beloved Richard. Because of your prayer, we've finally been able to come."

I don't know what to say, so I let Marjorie continue explaining. "While praying, you were so open to Junior that he could visit you during the surgery and let you know you'd be okay. Now that you've opened your heart to us, we can share with you and our dear Richard how marvelous it is to have the gift of heaven."

After Marjorie and I talk for a while—there's so much I want to know about her—Junior tenderly touches my face. "We want you to know that families can be together in heaven for eternity."

I shake my head in disbelief and whisper, "Really? How?" Though having a family in heaven seems impossible, so does seeing Richard's dearly departed family. The love I feel from them makes me giddy with joy. I don't want this feeling to ever end. I don't want to ever wake up.

Yet I have to. Someone is shaking my shoulders.

"Jane, sweetie, how are you feeling?" Richard asked as he gently touched my shoulder.

"Oh, I had the most wonderful dream, Richard," I answered sleepily. "I saw your dad again, and he brought his dad and your mom."

Excited to describe the dream, I sat up, propping myself against a pillow. "I love your mom. She has so much energy, and she loves you so much! I feel like we know each other so well already. She loves the music from *Oklahoma*; she eats corn on the cob like a typewriter; and when she wakes up in the morning, she stretches just like a cat."

By this time, Richard's mouth was hanging open. But I didn't stop. I couldn't. I was still enraptured in the experience. "She's beautiful and smells delightful. I asked her what perfume she wears, and she said it's your favorite: White Shoulders."

Stunned, Richard rubbed his face. I kept talking a mile a minute, so excited to share what I'd learned about his family. Finally, I paused for breath, and Richard asked, "Honey, are you feeling okay? Do you need another pain pill?" He looked more worried than he'd been before I went in for surgery.

I rolled my eyes. "No, I had a pill about two hours ago. Did you hear what I said? I dreamed about your mom. She showed me her greenhouses with all the orchids, and she made me feel like a treasured daughter."

Richard's eyes filled with tears as he whispered, "Jane, what can this mean? How can this be real? My mom died before I met you, and I've never told you about her. But you're describing her as if she were standing right here."

He started sobbing, and he enveloped me in his arms.

"Richard, do you believe in my dreams?"

He squeezed my hand. "Yes. With every ounce of my soul." Then a look of concern crossed his face. "I just hope your dreams of my family continue."

And continue they did. For two months after the surgery, I was confined to bed and slept a lot—my body needed the rest to heal. I came to love sleep because it meant I would get to see Richard's and my family, to learn more about them, to see heaven, and to feel of God's love.

Because of what I've learned and shared with Richard, we've embarked on a new, joyful journey in life and look forward to the day we'll be able to be with our family in heaven.

At first, the journey was personal. But in 2011, I felt a calling to share my story with others so they can be blessed just as I've been. In fact, the first time Richard's mother visited me, she told me, "When the time is right, you'll share this story. You'll know your day to spread His word has arrived."

The day Marjorie spoke of has come, and now I'm filled with a continuous desire to share God's message of love with everyone I meet. I've written this book as a way to share with you what I've learned about God, His gospel, and heaven. And, of course, families—after all, that's what God and heaven are all about.[1] In the following chapters, I invite you to come with me on my journey. This is a journey of the sweetest dreams possible. Dreams that will help you feel God's encompassing love. Embrace the joy that comes from learning the lessons of heaven.

NOTE

1. Though I've had numerous dreams, I don't think I'll ever forget any one of them. They're all so vivid. As for the details, Richard has ensured I won't forget them: he has written down the specifics of every dream I've described to him. At first, I didn't understand why he was doing it, but then he explained that what I was describing—his beloved family members, heaven, and Jesus Christ—was so precious that he wanted to be able to review it for the rest of his life. Years later, he continues to record my experiences.

Chapter 2

My Dreams Are Real

You aren't unique in having this gift, Jane, just blessed to see it so clearly."

Marjorie spoke those words the first time I saw her in a dream. I don't know all the reasons why I have the gift of dreams and why most other people don't. Why not Richard, since it was his family who first reached out to us from heaven? While I can't answer that question, I do know that each person on the earth receives at least one gift of the Spirit (see D&C 46:11).[1] We can use our gifts when we exercise faith, so perhaps I had activated my gift by reaching out to Heavenly Father in prayer the night before the surgery.

Though Richard doesn't have the gift of dreams, he does have the gift of belief. He accepted the truth of my dreams even before I did. For quite a while, I thought the dreams were the result of my wearied body and pain medication. Sure, I experienced the dreams, but they were fleeting and seemed too good to be true. I wondered whether Richard was telling me family stories before I fell asleep and then the stories were weaving into my dreams. He assured me he wasn't; he confidently told me there was no way that I could know so many details about his family unless the dreams were real. In fact, in the many dreams I've had over the years, I've never gotten a detail wrong. I've even been able to tell Richard details he didn't know.

During one dream, Marjorie showed me a faded photograph of a young Richard wearing a cowboy outfit. Marjorie explained that he simply loved that outfit and would wear it over and over again. He never noticed that as he grew, so did the outfit, matching him length for length. The source of the magic was Marjorie, who quietly and lovingly reworked her son's outfit three times so he could continue wearing his favorite duds. When I revealed this information to Richard, tears of gratitude streamed down his face—both for his mother and for having heard this story of her love for him.

Another time, I dreamed that before Richard's grandmother died, she moved from Hawaii to Ohio. Richard was again surprised—he thought his grandma had died in Hawaii. He was quite adamant that she had lived her entire life there. Unsure, I asked, "Are you positive? In the dream, she was in a nursing home in Ohio." Sure enough, after some research, we found her death record—in Ohio. She'd moved there, where one of her sons lived, shortly before her death.

After another dream, I woke up and asked Richard if he knew about the servant, Violet Ishamura, who had worked at his grandparents' house. Richard was skeptical, saying his grandparents would never have had a servant. He thought maybe this once I'd misunderstood my dream, and so he decided to prove it. During his search, he checked the 1930 census. It just so happened that the entry for his grandparents indicated a servant was part of the household. We were both amazed to learn that I was right.

The gift of belief and the gift of conversing with angels are both mentioned in Moroni chapter 10. Verse 11 talks about having the gift of "exceedingly great faith," while verse 14 describes the gift of "the beholding of angels and ministering spirits." We also learn in this chapter that "all these gifts come by the Spirit of Christ" to profit all humankind. I take that to mean that we shouldn't deny these gifts when we receive them (see Moroni 10:8, 17). Richard and I have both tried to accept the gifts we've received, which is one reason I'm sharing my experience in this book.

Richard and I have come to embrace our gifts. Every day, we thank our incredible, generous God for the spiritual gifts He has bestowed upon us. We also strive to use them for the benefit of others.

Some other members of my family, including my brother and sister, also have the gift of seeing angels, though not as frequently.

And I've heard many stories of other people who've been blessed by seen and unseen angels. Maybe you, like Richard, have the gifts of faith and compassion. Or maybe you have one of the many other gifts listed in the scriptures, particularly 1 Corinthians 12, Moroni 10, and Doctrine and Covenants 46. These gifts include prophesying, healing, speaking in tongues, interpreting tongues, acquiring and sharing wisdom, and discerning spirits (see 1 Corinthians 12:8–10; Moroni 10:9–16; and D&C 46:13–26).

Two gifts not explicitly stated in 1 Corinthians 12, Moroni 10, and Doctrine and Covenants 46 are the twin abilities of recognizing and following the promptings of the Spirit. Though not mentioned by name, these gifts are important for all of us to develop—and God has said that we all can (see John 14:26; D&C 8:1–4; 9:8–9).[2] I realize that recognizing the Spirit's voice may seem mystical, too intangible, and uncontrollable, but there really are steps we can take to tune in. Critical components include keeping God's commandments, exercising faith in Christ, and searching the scriptures.[3] We should also avoid strong negative emotions, such as anger, pride, jealousy, and defensiveness.[4] As Elder Richard G. Scott warned, "When such influences are present, it is like trying to savor the delicate flavor of a grape while eating a jalapeño pepper. Both flavors are present, but one completely overpowers the other. In like manner, strong emotions overcome the delicate promptings of the Holy Spirit."[5]

In contrast, a sense of humor—a happy humor, not one based on making fun of or feeling better than others—can help us feel the Spirit. While we're at it, if we want to improve our spiritual antennae, we should get enough sleep, exercise regularly, and eat nutritious foods.[6]

And we must always be listening—listening very carefully, in fact, because the Spirit usually whispers. Rarely will the Holy Ghost shout or even speak at a normal conversation level (see 1 Kings 19:12). Although listening so carefully takes a lot of effort on our part, it makes sense that the Holy Ghost usually speaks quietly. After all, He's the comforter, and I don't feel much comfort or peace when someone is yelling at me.

Listening isn't always an easy thing to do in our fast-paced world filled with noise 24/7 (one of the downsides, in my opinion, of modern technology). If we're always on the run, always watching something on YouTube, and always checking out friends' Facebook posts—sometimes we try to do all three at the same time!—then the noise is going to drown out whatever the Spirit is trying to tell us. We might tell ourselves that we're listening, but I've heard teenagers say the same thing when they're playing a video game and supposedly also listening to what their parents are saying. I don't buy it. If we don't set aside time each week—or, even better, each day—to be still and listen to the Holy Ghost, we'll likely miss out on a lot of what He wants to share with us. As LaNae Valentine said, "That quiet, still place must extend to our state of mind. The Spirit has difficulty impressing a busy, racing, anxious mind." Even if we're doing everything else we need to in order to hear the Spirit, if we don't make time to stop and listen, we'll likely miss a lot of what the Holy Ghost wants to share with us.[7]

Take a moment to think about the noise in your life and whether it's distracting you from hearing the Holy Ghost. If you see some room for improvement, decide right now what you're going to do to reduce the noise. I'm serious about this, and I want you to follow through. So write your action steps below. Make sure to be specific—and realistic. Then share your action items with someone to create accountability.

_____

_____

_____

_____

_____

Another thing we need to do is ask. As Jesus promised, "Ask, and ye shall receive" (John 16:24; 3 Nephi 27:29). I like that we find the same promise in Matthew 21:22 but also the reminder that we must ask in *faith*: "And all things, whatsoever ye shall ask in prayer, believing, ye shall receive." If we don't really believe we'll receive guidance from the Holy Spirit, we probably won't. Or, if the Holy Ghost does provide it, we likely won't be in tune, so we'll miss the message. But when we ask in faith, expecting an answer to come, we're more likely to listen and we'll be ready to receive inspiration when it comes.[8]

So how do we know when the Holy Ghost is talking to us? How do we know a thought is from the Holy Ghost and not just something we've come up with ourselves? A big indicator is how we feel. Does the idea bring us peace, happiness, confidence, or excitement?[9] If so, then the idea is likely from the Holy Ghost. Or, the idea may be ours, but the Holy Ghost is confirming that it's good and aligns with God's plans for us. I've heard people say that whenever an idea comes into our mind to do something nice, we should do it—immediately! It doesn't really matter whether the thought came directly from the Holy Ghost or whether a Christlike thought came to us of our own accord. Anything that is uplifting is ultimately of God, so we can be confident it's good and should be followed. And as we follow these promptings and ideas, we'll likely start to notice more of them. Not just once a month or once a week but every day. Even several times a day! That will happen because we're becoming better at recognizing the Spirit's promptings.[10] I like what LaNae Valentine said about learning to recognize the Spirit's whisperings in our lives: "Growing in our ability to receive revelation [another term for the Spirit's whisperings] is like learning a new language or learning to play a musical instrument. We must practice diligently for a long time before we feel comfortable with it. We must be patient with ourselves, recognize that we might have some setbacks, and persist until we become masters at recognizing a witness of the Spirit."[11]

Now, what thoughts aren't from the Holy Ghost? Again, let's consider how the thoughts make us feel. What ideas make us think we're better than others or encourage us to do something we know is wrong? When those ideas come, I certainly don't feel happy, peaceful, or loving, and that's a sure sign that the ideas aren't from the Holy Ghost.

Richard and I have both increased our sensitivity to the Holy Ghost's messages for us. Hearing the Spirit has come easier to me than to Richard, owing to my experiences talking with heavenly angels. Because of my spiritual gift, I've known at the very moment when family members have passed away. I knew when my mother, who lived across the country, needed someone to check on her health. I knew when my dad broke his back. I've also received promptings when friends have needed help. More than once, the Spirit has kept Richard and me from danger. For example, one day as I was riding my bike, the Spirit told me to stop. I quickly braked, and the next moment a car zoomed by, right where I would have been riding.

On another occasion, Richard and I were driving when I suddenly yelled out, "Slow down! There's a deer coming." Sure enough, the deer appeared on the road in front of us. Because Richard had responded to my warning, we were going slow enough by then that we were able to avoid hitting the deer.

At another time, while Richard and I were in Arkansas for a book tour, a tornado struck. Inside our motorhome, we could hear the trees whipping about and thought they were going to fall on us. The Holy Ghost whispered that we should take shelter in the bathroom. A while later, I felt a prompting that we should drive to a nearby spot along the Arkansas River. We took shelter there until the tornado dissipated. I'm not sure what would have happened to us if we'd ignored the promptings, but based on the damage the tornado caused to the area, the outcome wouldn't have been good.

The Holy Ghost was also the reason we were on a book tour. I'd received a strong prompting that I needed to write a book about my dreams and that I then should go on a promotional tour.[12] Many times during the writing process, the Spirit told me what to include in the book. The Spirit then told me where to go during the tour. The book tour was a critical step in Richard's and my journey to achieving an eternal family, as Junior had said was possible. That journey has led us to read the holy scriptures, and the Holy Ghost has increased our understanding of what we read. The Holy Ghost has even taught me more about myself. For one, I've learned that I'm much stronger than I thought I was—I can handle hard things, including multiple surgeries and illnesses that have landed me in the ICU.

Although Richard's ability to recognize the Spirit was slower in coming, he's always had the faith to believe in the promptings I've received. Over time, that faith has helped him recognize the Spirit when it speaks to him. I can think of many examples, but I'll share just one. On a beautiful day in California's Santa Barbara State Park, where we were camping, Richard decided to go fishing.

"Do you want to come with me, Jane?"

"I'm not feeling that great, so I'll just stay here," I responded. "Which spot are you going to?"

Shrugging, Richard replied, "The usual one down at the cove."

At that moment I had a thought that was mine but wasn't mine. "Don't go there. Try Harvey's Cove instead. When you get there, go down the stairs, turn to your right, and then fish right there."

Richard cocked his head to the left and asked, "Do you have a feeling?"

I simply smiled and kissed him goodbye. Then Richard headed toward the cove. I had no doubt Richard would bring back a fish or two. But I wasn't prepared for the total joy I saw on his face when he returned. "Come see what I caught!" Then he held up the biggest catfish I've ever seen. "You were right. The cove is a terrific fishing spot!"

Since that special day, Richard has shared with me thoughts that he knows have come from the Holy Ghost. He follows these ideas, just as he's had faith to act on the thoughts that have come to me. And that has blessed both of us. For instance, a while back I had oral surgery, and the pain afterward was excruciating. All I'd been given by the surgeon was extra-strength Tylenol, and that wasn't doing anything to relieve the agony. Richard was at a loss for what to do, but then the Holy Ghost prompted him to give me a special blessing, even telling Richard the words to say. Heeding the Spirit, Richard commanded the pain to go away—and it did, almost immediately! And, to my amazement, it didn't return. (I learned that sincere prayers guided by the Spirit can be the best painkiller.)

Because of this and the many other experiences we've had, we always strive to listen to the Spirit's whisperings, and we're not afraid to follow the counsel we receive. We know that doing so brings about the best good for us, as well as for those around us.

Find within yourself the faith to recognize the gifts that make you a special part of Heavenly Father's plan. Don't be afraid to ask God to reveal your gifts to you.[13] I love what President Henry B. Eyring has said: "God knows our gifts. My challenge to you and to me is to pray to know the gifts we have been given, to know how to develop them, and to recognize the opportunities to serve others that God provides us."[14] If you doubt whether God will answer your prayer, remember what Christ promised: "Ask, and it shall be given you; seek, and ye shall find; knock, and it shall be opened unto you: For every one that asketh receiveth; and he that seeketh findeth; and to him that knocketh it shall be opened" (Matthew 7:7–8).

I know He will bless you with gifts—and the ability to use them. Part of our purpose in mortality is to develop gifts of the Spirit and to apply them to move forward God's grand work. To contribute to Heavenly Father's plan, we shouldn't limit ourselves to praying to recognize and use our own talents. We should also "help others discover their special gifts from God," enabling them to serve along with us.[15]

Whatever your gifts may be, take this opportunity to learn and benefit from mine. Then work on developing your own gifts, so you can be more filled with the Spirit and help those around you as well (see D&C 46:9–26).

Notes

1. In the following pages, you'll see many references to scriptures in the Book of Mormon, Doctrine and Covenants, and Pearl of Great Price. If you aren't familiar with these scriptural compilations, refer to chapter 7 for an introduction to them.
2. See also David M. McConkie, "Learning to Hear and Understand the Spirit," *Ensign,* February 2011.

3. James E. Faust, "Voice of the Spirit," *Ensign,* June 2006. I've also fine-tuned my ability to hear the Spirit by frequently attending the temple and completing ordinances for family members.
4. Richard G. Scott, "How to Obtain Revelation and Inspiration for Your Personal Life," *Ensign,* May 2012; Richard G. Scott, "To Acquire Spiritual Guidance," *Ensign,* November 2009.
5. Scott, "To Acquire Spiritual Guidance."
6. Scott, "How to Obtain Revelation and Inspiration for Your Personal Life."
7. LaNae Valentine, "Discerning the Will of the Lord for Me" (Brigham Young University devotional, June 29, 2004), 4, speeches.byu.edu; see also Boyd K. Packer, "Reverence Invites Revelation," *Ensign,* November 1991.
8. Scott, "How to Obtain Revelation and Inspiration for Your Personal Life."
9. Scott, "How to Obtain Revelation and Inspiration for Your Personal Life"; Valentine, "Discerning the Will of the Lord for Me."
10. David A. Bednar, "That We May Always Have His Spirit to Be with Us," *Ensign,* May 2006.
11. Valentine, "Discerning the Will of the Lord for Me."
12. The first book is titled *What Heaven Is Like* (2012). While that book does outline some of my dreams and various aspects of heaven, the focus is on what I learned about Richard's family.
13. I encourage Latter-day Saints who have received a patriarchal blessing to read through it, looking for gifts of the Spirit. You'll likely find at least one.
14. Henry B. Eyring, "Help Them Aim High," *Ensign,* November 2012.
15. Eyring, "Help Them Aim High."

Chapter 3

HEAVEN: THE GIFT

The first time I met Junior, he opened the door to heaven only slightly, explaining I wasn't ready for more right then. As I've continued to spend time with Richard's family in my dreams, the door has been opened wider and wider and I've experienced heaven for myself. Before, I had a completely different perception of what the afterlife would be like. I thought heaven was filled with angels who sat around all day, not doing much aside from praising God. They certainly weren't with their family members, and they weren't doing all of the exciting, enjoyable, and productive activities I now know go on in heaven. Frankly, before my first venture into heaven, I wasn't very excited to go there after dying. Floating around on a cloud while playing a harp didn't seem like something I wanted to do for *eternity*. I wasn't quite sure what about heaven made it so heavenly. But now I know. I've come to learn that heaven is all about family. And ice cream.[1]

The food in heaven is to die for (no pun intended). Seriously though, it's delicious. Each time you take a bite of something, it tastes as good as the first time you tried it. Another great tidbit: you can eat what you want, when you want, and you'll never gain weight!

Because everyone in heaven has a perfect body, they don't have to worry about high cholesterol, heart disease, and other physical illnesses. They're also free of the mental and emotional issues that plague us mortals.[2] I suppose people have different opinions of what a perfect body is. I'm not sure of God's criteria, but I know that in Junior's case, he went from being short and wearing glasses in mortality to being tall and having 20/20 vision in heaven. He doesn't look a day over twenty, his muscles are well defined, and his skin is bronze, as it was when he spent hours surfing as a young man. To him, that's when his body was at its prime, so that's what he looks like in heaven. Richard's mom prefers to look a little older—around thirty—and she too is physically perfect. Everyone in heaven is attractive, which makes sense since their bodies are free of any flaws. But there's more to it than that. They radiate a brilliant light, and their eyes—beautiful blues, browns, and greens—are piercing, as if they can look into your soul.

The most wonderful part of heaven—aside from feeling Jesus Christ's never-ending love—is all the time focused on family. Family members are always spending time together, and they hold parades, birthday parties, and other celebrations.[3] Every year right after Jesus's birthday, all of Richard's family goes to Grandma and Grandpa Powers's home for the biggest party of the year. And the celebrations aren't only for heavenly events; angels like to celebrate for us too. When they see that a grandchild on earth has a new tooth, they pull out the party favors. When a nephew earns his bachelor's degree, they set off fireworks.[4]

Celebrations with extended family are easy to hold because each family lives in a mansion. Family members' mansions are close by. For example, Richard's parents and grandparents live next door to each other. Yet at the same time—as is only possible in heaven—the mansions are located in the places we love the most: Richard's Grandma and Grandpa Powers live in Wisconsin, while Junior and Marjorie live by a cove in Hawaii—most of the time. When they're in the mood to ski, they walk outside and see snow slopes, which I don't think Hawaii is known for. (Best of all, in my opinion, is that the temperature doesn't feel freezing and no one falls when swooshing down the slopes). Even if you like seemingly contradictory places, it works out in heaven. Take, for example, Richard's aunt. Behind her mansion is a stunning lake; one half is brimming with glistening water, while the other half is frozen so she can go ice skating whenever she wants.

Each mansion is jaw dropping in beauty and comfort. In comparison, Bill Gates's estate in Washington, which cost $63 million to build, looks like a shack.[5] One reason for the beauty of the mansions—and heaven in general—is that all colors are much more intense than they are on earth. Autumn leaves are a vivid ruby red. Grass is a deep emerald green (with no sprinklers required!). Every color emanates a light that's hard to describe but that I know is somehow connected to the light that originates with God and Jesus Christ.

The best thing about the mansions is that each is filled with the things the owners love. Whoever started the rumor that "you can't take it with you" got it wrong. When we get to heaven, in our mansions we'll find those things that we cherished in life: letters, photographs, family keepsakes . . . the things that are really meaningful. And those things aren't typically the ones that get the big bucks in our imperfect mortal world. People in heaven are much better judges of value than people are on earth. For years, Richard's mom carried around a photograph of Richard as a child, wearing his beloved cowboy outfit. As I've visited with her in heaven, I've seen her carrying that same picture. That's the type of possession that's truly valued in heaven. Another fabulous discovery I've made about heavenly mansions is that when you need something, it's there. It's kind of like Mary Poppins pulling things out of a bottomless bag. When Richard's mom is making delicious meals, the ingredients are always an arm's reach away—no running to the store ever needed.

Heaven is also about what brings us personal delight. For me, it's having a front-row seat at an Elvis Presley concert—and somehow, every fan gets the best seat in the house. Perhaps your idea of bliss isn't watching the King perform. (Or maybe developing a love for Elvis happens to everyone when they are loosed from their mortal imperfections . . .) Whatever you enjoy, you'll be able to do it. Richard's mom loved whistling, and now she's the best whistler in heaven. If you love running, you'll be able to run farther or faster than you ever could in mortality. You'll also be able to spend time pursuing new interests.

You'll even be able to do the things you can't do now with your mortal body. For me, that means I'll be able to do flips, double tucks, and other gymnastic moves. Maybe you've always wanted to be a singer. Well, in heaven, you got it. You'll be able to sing with the purest, sweetest voice, giving today's rock stars a run for their money! Richard's mom loved ice skating while on earth, but after she dislocated her shoulder, her ice skating days were over . . . until she reached heaven. Now she ice skates all the time, while Richard's dad fishes—on the other half of the lake.[6]

Heaven is also a place of learning—not the boring, fall-asleep kind but the fun, exciting, and fulfilling kind. In my mortal state, I run away when I hear someone even mention the word *statistics*; the word *calculus* makes me shudder. Numbers and equations just aren't my thing. But in heaven, it's different. Learning still takes work, but our ability to learn will be so much greater. We'll learn things faster and in more depth. The concepts that seem incomprehensible to us today will make sense in heaven, and we'll be able to use our knowledge to do things we never thought possible (like racing space-ships around Saturn!).[7] I recently found a description of this process: "Instead of thinking in one channel, knowledge will rush in from all quarters; it will come in light like the light which flows from the sun, penetrating every part, informing the spirit, and giving understanding concerning ten thousand things at the same time; and the mind will be capable of receiving and retaining all."[8] We'll use this knowledge to fulfill our potential, which is to become more like God![9]

Heaven is also heavenly because everyone there feels so much less regret than we mortals do. They are trying to become more like God—more patient, more loving, more wise—and they don't have all the distractions of our fallen world, so they don't make all the mistakes that we do, especially when interacting with family (the ones we mortals sometimes have the hardest time treating kindly). And that's one reason everyone in heaven is so happy and bursting with energy in everything they do.

Since God loves us so much, the things we love during life will be with us when we reach heaven. That includes our pets. Animals (and all other living things) have spirits (see D&C 77:2), and when they die they go to heaven too.[10] Just as we'll celebrate upon reuniting with family members, we'll also rejoice when seeing our pets in heaven.

Because Richard and I now know that all living things have spirits—and that God loves them all—we're much more in tune with nature. We now stop to move worms off the running and biking path by our home, and Richard stopped fishing so he wouldn't hurt the fish. These are personal decisions Richard and I have made; I'm not suggesting you need to do the same. However, respecting nature has helped Richard and me to come closer to the Holy Ghost, hear His direction in our lives, and feel greater love for all forms of life.[11]

I now understand why going to heaven is a blessing, something we should strive to be worthy of and should look forward to (see Titus 3:7). Entering heaven is like arriving at a huge family reunion: you're greeted by crowds of people you love and who love you—even the ones you only vaguely recognize . . . or don't know at all. And don't worry—there's none of the awkwardness that we sometimes feel at earthly reunions.[12]

During one of my visits with Junior, he told me about his experience dying. He'd been lying in a hospital bed, and all of a sudden he was somehow above his body and looking down on it. Then he saw his parents, grandparents, and other relatives. "What are you all doing here?" he asked. In an instant he understood, as they greeted him and led him through the door of heaven. Family members who are already in heaven know when another relative is soon to cross the veil, and they are excitedly waiting to help the person make the transition. Instead of death being a scary, painful experience that involves traveling through a long, dark tunnel, it's an exhilarating experience filled with love and joy at seeing relatives we've been separated from.[13]

Because heaven is filled with families, love, and God's glory, God wants all of His children to qualify for heaven. For those who don't have the opportunity to accept Christ during mortal life, God gives them the opportunity after dying.[14] So, in addition to all the fun people have in heaven, they also spend time teaching family members, friends, and everyone else about the Savior and His Atonement.

What I learned is supported by these scripture verses I later found:

But behold, from among the righteous, he organized his forces and appointed messengers, clothed with power and authority, and commissioned them to go forth and carry the light of the gospel to them that were in darkness, even to all the spirits of men; and thus was the gospel preached to the dead. . . . Thus was the gospel preached to those who had died in their sins, without a knowledge of the truth, or in transgression, having rejected the prophets. (D&C 138:30, 32)

In heaven, there are also opportunities to serve, including by helping us here on earth. I believe that it's the combination of missionary work and gospel teaching, service, and family activities that truly makes heaven a glorious place.[15]

When I think of heaven, I feel the immense love of deceased family and our Savior, Jesus Christ. My heart is so full, I wish I could share my knowledge from the rooftops!

Because of my visions of heaven, I'm no longer afraid of death. Neither is Richard. We now understand that heaven is a place of love, family, and joy. If you've seen heaven as I have, you know it's a place of glory you never want to leave. Doctrine and Covenants 42:46 explains it well: "Those that die in me shall not taste of death, for it shall be sweet unto them."

While being in heaven is always wonderful, I also have greater joy and hope in my life on earth.[16] I no longer beg Richard's father to let me stay in heaven with him. I know that my life here has purpose, and there's much to be grateful for and to enjoy. There's also much I still need to learn and ways in which I need to grow and become better.

While life on earth is certainly a time of testing, trials, and struggles, God also intends for us to experience great happiness, moments of exhilaration, the sweetness of relationships, and the confidence that comes from conquering challenges (see 2 Nephi 2:25). I realize that during our trials, it can be hard to remember the times of peace and happiness that we've felt in the past and that we're sure to experience in the future. But if we'll remember the help and comfort we've received in the past—and ask the Lord for help—persevering through our troubles will be easier. Remember the Savior's promise: "Come unto me, all ye that labour and are heavy laden, and I will give you rest. Take my yoke upon you, and learn of me; for I am meek and lowly in heart: and ye shall find rest unto your souls. For my yoke is easy, and my burden is light" (Matthew 11:28–30).

When Christ makes a promise, He keeps it. Notice that in the scripture above, He didn't say that He'd remove the burden. I've found that to be the case many times in my life. Though I may plead to be removed from a stressful situation, He has rarely taken me out of it; rather, He's taken on part of the load, making the situation easier for me to bear. Sometimes, He's also given me greater strength so that I can continue moving under a heavy burden.

President Dieter F. Uchtdorf acknowledged, "From time to time our lives may seem to be touched by, or even wrapped in, darkness. Sometimes the night that surrounds us will appear oppressive, disheartening, and frightening." When that's the case, reflect on the following insight from President Uchtdorf:

> Even though we may feel lost in the midst of our current circumstances, God promises the hope of His light—He promises to illuminate the way before us and show us the way out of darkness. . . .
>
> I repeat a wonderful and certain truth: God's light is real. It is available to all! It gives life to all things. It has the power to soften the sting of the deepest wound. It can be a healing balm for the loneliness and sickness of our souls. In the furrows of despair, it can plant the seeds of a brighter hope. It can enlighten the deepest valleys of sorrow. It can illuminate the path before us and lead us through the darkest night into the promise of a new dawn.
>
> This is "the Spirit of Jesus Christ," which gives "light to every man that cometh into the world."[17]

Now, how do we gain access to the Spirit of Jesus Christ and His light? We have to do our part—we have to take action. As President Uchtdorf counseled, "Spiritual light rarely comes to those who merely sit in darkness waiting for someone to flip a switch." President Uchtdorf described three critical steps in receiving this light:

- Start where we are. It's never too early or too late. We don't have to wait until we become better people than we think we are right now.
- Turn our hearts toward Jesus Christ. We need to talk to Him as we would a friend—because He is! It's also important to talk to Heavenly Father in prayer. We can tell Him about our struggles. He will listen. Then we can ask Him to help us see His light and hear His gentle voice in our lives.
- Walk in Christ's light. As frustrating or defeating as it may feel, we all make mistakes. When we acknowledge that fact and then repent through a belief in the Atonement, we are inviting Christ's light into our lives. That light will bring us joy and will also lessen our desire to sin.

When we follow these steps, we nurture our hope in Christ that He can help lift our burdens and make life more bearable. President Uchtdorf concluded:

> I bear witness that our living hope is in Christ Jesus! He is the true, pure, and powerful entrance to divine enlightenment.
>
> I testify that with Christ, darkness cannot succeed. Darkness will not gain victory over the light of Christ.
>
> I bear witness that darkness cannot stand before the brilliant light of the Son of the living God!
>
> I invite each of you to open your heart to Him. Seek Him through study and prayer.
>
> Brothers and sisters, even after the darkest night, the Savior of the world will lead you to a gradual, sweet, and bright dawn that will assuredly rise within you.
>
> As you walk toward the hope of God's light, you will discover the compassion, love, and goodness of a loving Heavenly Father, "in [whom there] is no darkness at all."[18]

But what about those who suffer in a seemingly impenetrable darkness, such as because of a mental illness? For some, the darkness is so overpowering that the idea of ending their time on mortality seems to be a welcome relief. My heart goes out to anyone who suffers from such a burden. Whatever the cause, if you or a loved one has contemplated suicide, I want to offer a message of hope. More accurately, I want to share the words of hope expressed by Elder Jeffrey R. Holland, who struggled with depression as a young father. I've chosen to use his words because he's more eloquent than I am and because I believe his words were inspired by God:

> In striving for some peace and understanding in these difficult matters [mental illnesses and emotional disorders], it is crucial to remember that we are living—and chose to live—in a fallen world where for divine purposes our pursuit of godliness will be tested and tried again and again. Of greatest assurance in God's plan is that a Savior was promised, a Redeemer, who through our faith in Him would lift us triumphantly over those tests and trials, even though the cost to do so would be unfathomable for both the Father who sent Him and the Son who came. It is only an appreciation of this divine love that will make our own lesser suffering first bearable, then understandable, and finally redemptive.

In addition to the hope that comes from believing in Christ's Atonement and Resurrection, Elder Holland encouraged us to "believe in miracles. I have seen so many of them come when every other indication would say that hope was lost. Hope is never lost. If those miracles do not come soon or fully or seemingly at all, remember the Savior's own anguished example: if the bitter cup does not pass, drink it and be strong, trusting in happier days ahead."

Elder Holland acknowledged that our belief in Christ and hope for miracles may not be enough: "If things continue to be debilitating, seek the advice of reputable people with certified training, professional skills, and good values. Be honest with them about your history and your struggles. Prayerfully and responsibly consider the counsel they give and the solutions they prescribe. If you had appendicitis, God would expect you to seek a priesthood blessing *and* get the best medical care available. So too with emotional disorders. Our Father in Heaven expects us to use *all* of the marvelous gifts He has provided in this glorious dispensation."

Even during the darkest days of our trials, whether physical, mental, or otherwise, we should look for things to be grateful for. There will always be something; if we look hard enough, Heavenly Father will help us recognize something to express gratitude about.

But I realize that the trials may seem to greatly outweigh the blessings. At such times, some people may believe that exiting this life is the best option. But Elder Holland exhorted that whatever the circumstance:

> Do not vote against the preciousness of life by ending it! Trust in God. Hold on in His love. Know that one day the dawn will break brightly and all shadows of mortality will flee. Though we may feel we are "like a broken vessel," as the Psalmist says, we must remember, that vessel is in the hands of the divine potter. Broken minds can be healed just the way broken bones and broken hearts are healed. While God is at work making those repairs, the rest of us can help by being merciful, nonjudgmental, and kind.
>
> I testify of the holy Resurrection, that unspeakable cornerstone gift in the Atonement of the Lord Jesus Christ! With the Apostle Paul, I testify that that which was sown in corruption will one day be raised in incorruption and that which was sown in weakness will ultimately be raised in power. I bear witness of that day when loved ones whom we knew to have disabilities in mortality will stand before us glorified and grand, breathtakingly perfect in body and mind. What a thrilling moment that will be![19]

I add my own testimony to Elder Holland's. I know that in heaven, our bodies will be perfect, no longer susceptible to illness of any kind. We'll be awed by the perfection of our bodies and profoundly grateful to be free of mortal frailties. But we'll also express appreciation for the imperfections of our mortal bodies—for all that we were able to do and for the refining lessons we learned as we grappled with our physical weaknesses.

NOTES

1. This chapter contains descriptions of heaven, as I've seen it. You may be skeptical of some of the activities I've watched—and participated in—during my heavenly dreams. I don't blame you. They definitely don't match most people's pictures of heaven. Keep in mind that God and Jesus Christ often use symbolism and metaphors to communicate truths (see, for example, Luke 22:19–20, the book of Revelation, and

Jacob 5). So, if you can't quite accept some of my depictions at face value, look a little deeper and see if you can identify the symbolism that may be at play in the fun heavenly activities that I describe.

2. I love this promise from Brigham Young: "Here, we are continually troubled with ills and ailments of various kinds, and our ears are saluted with the expressions, 'My head aches,' 'My shoulders ache,' 'My back aches,' 'I am hungry, dry, or tired;' but in the spirit world we are free from all this and enjoy life, glory, and intelligence" (In *Journal of Discourses* [London: Latter-Day Saints' Book Depot], 14:231).

3. It shouldn't be surprising to Latter-Day Saints that angels engage in many of the activities we engage in during mortality. Doctrine and Covenants 130:2 explains that we're eternally social beings and that the "same sociality which exists among us here will exist among us there, only it will be coupled with eternal glory, which glory we do not now enjoy."

4. Jedediah M. Grant, who served in the First Presidency from 1854 to 1856, had a near-death experience, during which he saw the spirit world. He later explained that the people there were organized into families, just as they are in mortality. (*Journal of Discourses*, 4:135–136.)

5. As Heber C. Kimball recounted, Jedediah M. Grant "spoke of the buildings he saw there, remarking that the Lord gave Solomon wisdom and poured gold and silver into his hands that he might display his skill and ability, and said that the temple erected by Solomon was much inferior to the most ordinary buildings he saw in the spirit world" (*Journal of Discourses*, 4:136).

6. As a side note, in heaven the fish don't mind being caught; it doesn't hurt them, and they're always released back into the water. It's like a game of hide-and-go-seek.

7. Brigham Young said that as we learn in heaven, we'll progress "from one intelligence and power to another, our happiness becoming more and more exquisite and sensible as we proceed in the words and powers of life" (*Discourses of Brigham Young*, ed. John A. Widtsoe [Salt Lake City, UT: Deseret Book, 1954], 379–380).

8. Orson Pratt, in *Journal of Discourses*, 2:246.

9. "Becoming Like God," The Church of Jesus Christ of Latter-day Saints, https://www.lds.org/topics/becoming-like-god.

10. Elder Bruce R. McConkie stated that the "power of the resurrection is universal in scope. Man, the earth, and all life thereon will come forth in the resurrection." (*Mormon Doctrine* [Salt Lake City, UT: Bookcraft, 1966], p. 642). Joseph Smith similarly asserted that animals will be

resurrected and will live in heaven. He presented this principle when discussing the beasts mentioned in Revelation chapter 5. Joseph Smith explained:

> John saw curious looking beasts in heaven; he saw every creature that was in heaven,—all the beasts, fowls and fish in heaven. . . .
>
> John learned that God glorified himself by saving all that his hands had made, whether beasts, fowls, fishes or men; and he will glorify himself with them.
>
> Says one, "I cannot believe in the salvation of beasts." Any man who would tell you that this could not be, would tell you that the revelations are not true. (*History of The Church of Jesus Christ of Latter-day Saints* [Salt Lake City, UT: Deseret News], 5:343.)

11. Though God has given humans dominion over all other forms of life, He's also given several indications that He wants us to treat them kindly. For instance, see Deuteronomy 22:6–7, 10; Luke 12:6; and Doctrine and Covenants 49:21. Many latter-day prophets have encouraged us to treat animals kindly. Several examples are cited in Gerald E. Jones, "The Gospel and Animals," *Ensign,* August 1972. One of these examples is from Joseph Smith:

> In pitching my tent we found three massasaugas or prairie rattlesnakes, which the brethren were about to kill, but I said, "Let them alone— don't hurt them! How will the serpent ever lose his venom, while the servants of God possess the same disposition, and continue to make war upon it? Men must become harmless, before the brute creation; and when men lose their vicious dispositions and cease to destroy the animal race, the lion and the lamb can dwell together, and the sucking child can play with the serpent in safety." . . . I exhorted the brethren not to kill a serpent, bird, or an animal of any kind during our journey unless it became necessary in order to preserve ourselves from hunger. (*History of The Church of Jesus Christ of Latter-day Saints* [Salt Lake City, UT: Deseret News], pp. 71–72.)

12. Brigham Young related, "We have more friends behind the veil than on this side, and they will hail us more joyfully than you were ever welcomed by your parents and friends in this world; and you will rejoice more when you meet them than you ever rejoiced to see a friend in this life" (*Discourses of Brigham Young,* 379–380).

13. See also Henry B. Eyring, "The Holy Ghost as Your Companion," *Ensign,* November 2015.

14. For more information on accepting Christ and qualifying for heaven, see chapters 7 and 8.

15. Brent L. Topp, professor of religious education at Brigham Young University and author of *What's on the Other Side? What the Gospel Teaches Us about the Spirit World,* said some people "may think that the only thing that goes on there is missionary work. I sometimes joke in my classes that if you find yourself in the spirit world being preached *to,* that's not a good sign. But we know that isn't true either. We will be teaching and being taught, serving and being served—just like here" (Devan Jensen, "What's on the Other Side? A Conversation with Brent L. Top on the Spirit World," *Religious Educator* 14, no. 2 (2013): 43–63).

16. My feelings echo Romans 15:13: "Now the God of hope fill you with all joy and peace in believing, that ye may abound in hope, through the power of the Holy Ghost." I explain the reason for my hope in chapter 6 of this book.

17. Dieter F. Uchtdorf, "The Hope of God's Light," *Ensign,* May 2013.

18. Uchtdorf, "The Hope of God's Light." For another message of hope centered in Jesus Christ, watch the video "Lifting Burdens" at https://www.lds.org/media-library/video/2009-10-38-lifting-burdens.

19. Jeffrey R. Holland, "Like a Broken Vessel," November 2013. If you or someone you know is contemplating suicide, please seek assistance. Valuable resources are available at suicidepreventionlifeline.org and lifelineforattemptsurvivors.org.

Chapter 4

HIS ARMS ENFOLD ME IN LOVE

I watch the man in reverence. No one needs to tell me it's Jesus. I just *know*. His eyes are a beautiful blue, and they're kind. Actually, *kind* is too tame a word to describe Jesus's eyes. They radiate love—but not just any love. It's a love that's purer, deeper, more encompassing than I'd ever felt before. Almost too much to understand. It's a love I can't adequately describe in words. But I have to try because I want you to experience what I've experienced.

Think of the person you love the most, and then multiply that love by ten—no, one hundred! Then imagine that love is transformed into a warm, soft blanket that's wrapped around you. In it you feel protected, peaceful, and secure. You feel *loved!* More than you ever thought possible. That's the closest I can come to describing Christ's love for each person—yes, including you.

In my dream, I continue watching Jesus, captivated. It seems that I could continue looking at Him forever, and I'd be happy. It's not just His eyes that convey His love; it's everything about Him. I'm awestruck that He's holding millions of children on His lap. Yet at the same time, it's as if He's only holding one because each child has His full attention and is feeling His complete love. I don't understand how it's possible, but I know it's real.[1]

Even though I'm not sitting on His knee—I'm looking through a door Junior has opened just a sliver—I can feel Jesus's love for me personally. I yearn to reach out to Him, to run to Him and never leave. But Junior shakes his head. "Jane, it's time to go."

I know he's right. Even though I don't want to leave, I know I need to return to my body and mortal life. To Richard. And, oh, I have so much to tell him.

Since that first time seeing Jesus in heaven, I've had many more opportunities to see Him in my dreams. Each time, it feels like I'm being engulfed in His strong yet gentle arms and that He's welcoming me home. I feel of His love and glory, and my heart overflows with joy.

I've learned so many things from seeing Jesus in heaven, and I want you to learn them too. First, I learned that Jesus is real! I grew up believing in Jesus, but He wasn't someone I knew. He was somewhat of an unknowable being, someone I couldn't really understand. He was far removed and intangible. It's important to note that He seemed distant because I kept Him that way. Christ stands at the door and knocks (see Revelation 3:20). But until we let Him in, He'll remain an outsider and a stranger to us. Because He loves us so much, He won't force Himself upon us. We must choose to invite Him into our lives. By doing so, we can come to know Him and how much He loves us.

But because I had not opened the door to Christ, it was easy to not consider Him a real, living person. So when Junior opened heaven's door for me, my eyes were opened to the fact that Jesus is real. The many Bible scriptures about Him are true. Here's a sampling:

- Malachi 1:2: "I have loved you, saith the Lord."
- Jeremiah 31:3: "The Lord hath appeared of old unto me, saying, Yea, I have loved thee with an everlasting love."
- John 15:9: "As the Father hath loved me, so have I loved you: continue ye in my love."
- Ephesians 5:2: "Christ also hath loved us, and hath given himself for us an offering and a sacrifice to God."

My discoveries about Jesus being real and loving everyone so much led to another discovery: He really did atone for our sins! Although I don't understand exactly how He was able to suffer for our sins, I do understand why He chose to: He loves us more than we can comprehend. He loves us so much that He was willing to bear unimaginable pain to redeem us all, even those who have abused and betrayed Him. The scriptures describe what Jesus's love led Him to do:

- Isaiah 53:3–5: "He is despised and rejected of men; a man of sorrows, and acquainted with grief: and we hid as it were our faces from him; he was despised, and we esteemed him not. Surely he hath borne our griefs, and carried our sorrows: yet we did esteem him stricken, smitten of God, and afflicted. But he was wounded for our transgressions, he was bruised for our iniquities: the chastisement of our peace was upon him; and with his stripes we are healed."

- Alma 7:11–13: "And he shall go forth, suffering pains and afflictions and temptations of every kind; and this that the word might be fulfilled which saith he will take upon him the pains and the sicknesses of his people. And he will take upon him death, that he may loose the bands of death which bind his people; and he will take upon him their infirmities, that his bowels may be filled with mercy, according to the flesh, that he may know according to the flesh how to succor his people according to their infirmities. Now the Spirit knoweth all things; nevertheless the Son of God suffereth according to the flesh that he might take upon him the sins of his people, that he might blot out their transgressions according to the power of his deliverance; and now behold, this is the testimony which is in me."

- Doctrine and Covenants 19:16–19: "For behold, I, God, have suffered these things for all, that they might not suffer if they would repent; but if they would not repent they must suffer even as I; which suffering caused myself, even God, the greatest of all, to tremble because of pain, and to bleed at every pore, and to suffer both body and spirit—and would that I might not drink the bitter cup, and shrink—nevertheless, glory be to the Father, and I partook and finished my preparations unto the children of men."

I can't fully comprehend being able to make such sacrifices, but because of my dreams, I know that Christ did accomplish His great work. His immeasurable love is the key—the element that motivated Him to press forward even when He asked God, "O my Father, if it be possible, let this cup pass from me" (Matthew 26:39).[2] His love for us didn't end when He finished atoning for our sins in the Garden of Gethsemane or when His crucified body was laid in the tomb or when He triumphantly rose from the grave. Perhaps His love for us even increased after the Atonement, just as we often develop a deeper love for the people we serve and sacrifice for. What I do know for certain is that Jesus's love is perfect and eternal.

One of the reasons I love my heavenly dreams so much is that I have the opportunity to bask in Jesus's radiant love. For the first while, after I woke up from my dreams I would crave to continue feeling Christ's love for me. Over time, I noticed a change. The love I felt in my dreams wasn't fading away after I awoke. I had been letting Christ enter my life, and I felt that love throughout the day. Now, it's a constant in my life. I feel His love so strongly that I can barely hold it in. I continually want to shout from the rooftops that Jesus loves me—and He loves you too!

His love is present at all times. However, I've learned that my thoughts and actions affect how strongly I feel His love. For instance, His love is less noticeable when I'm watching TV. In contrast, the intensity of the love I feel increases when I share my dreams with others, when I tell them about Christ's love, and when I'm serving others. The feeling of love starts in my chest and spreads throughout my body, all the way to my fingernails and the hairs on my head. The joy I feel almost overwhelms me.

I also experience His love more strongly in certain locations. Hospitals and rest homes are two places that Jesus's love is particularly powerful. The outdoors is another location that is bursting with Christ's love. I can feel His love in every blooming flower, chirping bird, and refreshing breeze.

Constantly feeling Jesus's love reminds me that He's aware of me and always ready to help me. Experiencing this love has also increased my love for Jesus, as well as for everyone I come in contact with. Particularly when I talk to people about my dreams, I'm blessed with a measure of His love for these people. With this love, I'm better able to know what to say to fill their hearts.

The love of Christ has also increased my belief in everything that is recorded in the scriptures and that Richard's family members have told me about the eternal nature of families. Further, Christ's love has given me insight into God's plan for His mortal children, particularly my role in that plan.

Seeing Christ and experiencing His continuous love have also helped me develop a relationship with God. I have never seen God in my dreams,[3] but I know He is also in heaven and loves me just as much as Jesus does. I've felt God's love for me and also believe the scriptures that talk of His love:

- 1 John 4:16: "God is love; and he that dwelleth in love dwelleth in God, and God in him."
- 1 John 4:10: "Herein is love, not that we loved God, but that he loved us, and sent his Son to be the propitiation for our sins."
- John 15:9: "As the Father hath loved me, so have I loved you: continue ye in my love."

The love that motivated and enabled Christ to suffer for our sins is the same love that motivated God to allow His perfect Son to suffer and die. God and Christ are one in love, just as they are one in purpose (see John 17:21).

As my understanding of and relationship with God increased, I began turning to Him in prayer more frequently and sincerely. Though I had previously prayed from time to time, I hadn't known how to really talk with God. As a child, I'd been taught rote prayers, but they limited my ability to share all my thoughts with God—my desires, my fears, and my gratitude. As I learned about His immense love for me, praying to Him in my own words became easier. I felt like I was talking with a dear friend who understands me completely—because He does!

When I pray, I feel His love and His presence. I know He's listening to me. I ask Him for guidance, and He willingly gives it, though not always immediately. He knows that sometimes I'm not ready for the answer or that I will have the opportunity to grow by patiently waiting for an answer. When the answer does come, I follow it, even if it's not the answer I'd hoped for. I know that, ultimately, His answer is the one that is best for me and will bring me the most happiness.

One morning, I asked Heavenly Father to help me have better health (I tend to get sick). I wanted Him to tell me that I should take a specific vitamin, eat a certain food, or maybe increase the distance I run each day. But His response wasn't something I expected . . . or honestly wanted. He told me to stop drinking energy drinks. I'd been having at least one a day and had come to rely on them. But when God told me I needed to stop, that's what I did. Though following that direction hasn't saved me from physical challenges, it has helped me recover from them when they come. I know that when we act on His answers, He blesses us. When we faithfully respond, it's also easier for us to hear His answer the next time we ask for guidance.

Because I've learned that God and Christ love me without limit, I've also learned to place my burdens on them and to let go of grief, pain, and anger. When people tell me about their trials, I feel the love that God and Christ have for these individuals. I also know that our Father in Heaven and Elder Brother don't want us to grieve. We can make trials much less stressful experiences and more valuable learning opportunities by shifting our focus. Instead of thinking about the challenges we're facing, we should stop and think about God and Christ. Focus on how much They love us, and then live in the moment of feeling Their love.

When I've felt overwhelmed, I've looked to Heavenly Father for assistance. "I put it into Thy hands," I tell Him. As I do, I feel His love encircling me, and the weight of the burden becomes lighter, more bearable. I can testify to the truthfulness of the Lord's promise: "And I will also ease the burdens which are put upon your shoulders, that even you cannot feel them upon your backs, even while you are in bondage" (Mosiah 24:14).[4]

I know that you can experience the same.

Notes

1. It's similar to Heavenly Father being able to hear all of the prayers around the world that are being said at one time. I don't know how He can hear your prayer while also listening to mine, but He can.

2. Interestingly—but not surprisingly, based on my heavenly experiences—when the Savior asked His Father to remove the bitter cup, "there appeared an angel unto him from heaven, strengthening him" (Luke 22: 43). God knew that removing the bitter cup wasn't for the ultimate good, so He sent an angel to minister unto Christ and help Him finish the mission that His love had motivated Him to begin.

3. I'm not sure why God doesn't appear in my dreams of heaven, but I have a few guesses. We have only a few accounts of God appearing to people on the earth (see The Guide to the Scriptures, s.v. "God, Godhead," lds.org/scriptures/gs/god-godhead). On the other hand, Jesus Christ lived on the earth and has appeared more frequently. That makes sense since He's the mediator between God and mortals and He represents God in all things (see 1 Timothy 2:5 and John 5:19). So it seems reasonable that I would only see Christ in my dreams. In John 14:9, Christ stated, "He that hath seen me hath seen the Father." Also, Doctrine and Covenants 76 indicates that only those who receive celestial glory will dwell in God's presence; those in the terrestrial glory will dwell in Christ's presence (see vv. 62 and 77).

Since I'm not yet ready for celestial glory, I'm likely not yet ready to see God.

4. See verse 15 for the fulfillment of this promise. See also Matthew 11:28–30.

Chapter 5

FAMILIES ARE ETERNAL

Richard's in agony. His twenty-year-old heart has just been broken: his girlfriend no longer wants to date him. He yearns for something to dull the pain, and alcohol seems the easiest fix. Soon, he's drunk. And reckless. He jumps on his motorcycle and speeds down the road, heading toward Palm Dale in San Fernando Valley. Even in his drunken haze, he knows he's going too fast. But he doesn't care.

I watch him in horror. I remind myself that it's a dream, that I'm seeing it all through the eyes of heaven. But I'm still afraid. Even if he weren't driving so fast, his impaired state and broken heart put him at serious risk of danger—both for himself and for other motorists. Because there's so much Richard hasn't told me about his younger years, I really don't know how this experience ends.

Slow down, Richard. Slow down!

He's about to take a sharp turn, and I freeze. But not because of fear. Rather, I'm shocked and then filled with overwhelming relief, gratitude, and love because I see two men holding onto Richard, steadying him on his bike and keeping him moving in a straight path. One of the men is Richard's dad, Junior. The other is Jesus. They continue to hold on to Richard until he makes it home.

Knowing that Richard's safe, Junior turns to me, tears running down his cheeks. Brushing away the tears, he says, "When you're in heaven, you can often see when family members are in danger. I saw Richard speed away, and I immediately prayed to God for help."

Wiping away another tear, Junior humbly murmurs, "My prayer was answered."

That dream was one of the most frightening I've had, aside from the occasional nightmare that we all experience. But even in this one, the lessons I learned are beautiful. First, I learned that even people in heaven pray to God. Their prayers are focused on helping family members who are still on earth—us. God hears these prayers and often allows our deceased loved ones to be part of the answer.[1]

Indeed, Joseph F. Smith explained, "Our fathers and mothers, brothers, sisters and friends who have passed away from this earth, having been faithful, and worthy to enjoy these rights and privileges, may have a mission given them to visit their relatives and friends upon the earth again, bringing from the divine Presence messages of love, of warning, or reproof and instruction, to those whom they had learned to love in the flesh."[2] Brigham Young stated that at least one reason angels play an important role in helping us is that God isn't physically everywhere, so he sends his angels and other agents, including prophets and apostles, to speak and act for Him.[3]

I later learned that God has sent angels to help His children on the earth since the very beginning, with Adam and Eve (see Moses 5:6–7). The Bible mentions angels visiting other people, including Abraham's wife Hagar, Jacob, Daniel, Elijah, Zechariah, Zacharias, and Mary the mother of Jesus.[4] Probably the most well-known visit from an angel was when the angel Gabriel visited the virgin Mary and told her that she would bear the Son of God.

What we may not remember (or have even known) is that angels visited our Savior. Since He's a God, in some ways it seems that He wouldn't need the help of angels while living on this earth, but He did—and not just once. After Jesus had fasted forty days and Satan tempted Him, "Angels came and ministered unto him" (Matthew 4:11). I think that ministering included providing strength and uplifting Him. Later, when Christ was suffering in Gethsemane and felt like the burden was more than He could handle, He once again was visited by an angel. The angel didn't remove Jesus from the situation—and didn't save Him from being crucified—but the angel did provide heavenly comfort, strengthening Christ to endure incomparable suffering (see Luke 22:43).

After Jesus Christ died and was resurrected, angels continued to appear to, strengthen, and teach people (see, for example, John 20:12 and Acts 5:19). And because God is an unchanging God and because we need the assistance of angels today just as much as did people in the Bible, angels continue to minister.

I've learned that when I pray out loud, angels (my deceased family members) are able to hear me and they'll start praying about the same thing. They've told me that they also get the word out about what I'm praying for, and soon, all of heaven is praying for me.[5] But we may not be aware of angels praying for us or coming to us in times of danger or sadness. Richard hadn't realized the heavenly protection he was blessed with that late night on the road. When I told him about my dream, tears welled in his eyes. "I always wondered how I made it home alive," he whispered. "Thank you, Dad. Thank you."[6]

Though we may not be aware of the angels watching over us, they are there. Brigham Young taught, "Can you see spirits in this room? No. Suppose the Lord should touch your eyes that you might see, could you then see the spirits? Yes, as plainly as you now see bodies, as did the servant of Elijah. If the Lord would permit it, and it was his will that it should be done, you could see the spirits that have departed from this world, as plainly as you now see bodies with your natural eyes."[7] And consider these thrilling words of Joseph F. Smith:

> We move and have our being in the presence of heavenly messengers and of heavenly beings. We are not separate from them. . . . We are closely related to our kindred, to our ancestors . . . who have preceded us into the spirit world. . . . We are associated and united to them by ties that we can not break. . . . Those who have been faithful, who have gone beyond . . . can see us better than we can see them; that they know us better than we know them. . . . They see us, they are solicitous for our welfare, they love us now more than ever. For now they see the dangers that beset us; . . . their love for us and their desire for our well being must be greater than that which we feel for ourselves.[8]

I believe that our family members in heaven are very involved in our daily lives, not just when we're in dire circumstances. Think about the last time you lost your keys and couldn't find them *anywhere*. But then, a few minutes later you found them on the counter in the exact spot you'd looked three times before. When that happens to me, I thank Heavenly Father and the departed family members who played a role in finding the keys for me.

Our deceased loved ones can also bring thoughts to our minds to communicate their love for us. On Christmas Eve several years ago, Richard was on his way home from work. He was weighed down with job-related problems and wasn't in the Christmas spirit. Actually, he hadn't been in the Christmas spirit since his youth—his dad had died during the holidays, and Richard had come to see Christmas as a bitter reminder of losing his best friend. So Richard was bemused when carol after carol popped into his head while driving home from a long day at the office. He didn't enjoy Christmas songs, let alone know their words, so how was it that he was singing them now? And then he knew. His mom *loved* Christmas: the music, the decorations, and everything in between. Looking up, he asked, "Mom, what are you doing? Why are you putting these songs in my head?" Though at first exasperated, quickly he felt loved. He knew his mom was sending him a message: he wouldn't be celebrating Christmas with his parents face to face, but they loved him immensely and wanted him to enjoy this special holiday. It was the best gift he received that year.

Richard also feels his mom with him when he hikes, reminding him of when they would hike together before she died. I think that such experiences are more common than most people realize.[9]

From the dream of Richard on his motorcycle, I also gained greater insight about God's marvelous plan for all of His children. While we grieve the deaths of those we love, we can also gain peace, comfort, and support knowing that their love for us continues and that they'll be watching over us and keeping us from harm's way—when that is God's will.[10] Their influence on us is magnified because they can communicate with us spirit to spirit. For example, Richard was protected the night of the motorcycle ride because Junior could see Richard's perilous circumstance and could provide the help needed— a type of help beyond the realm of mortals.

Junior had many motivations to keep his son safe that night— as well as on many other occasions. Richard's reckless driving could have injured or killed other drivers. If that had happened, guilt would have been his constant companion for the remainder of his life. He also could have lost his own life. Though I've learned that heaven is a wonderful place and I no longer fear dying, mortality is a precious phase of eternal life and should be treasured. Our bodies are temples and should be treated with respect and safeguarded from careless harm that invites premature death (see 1 Corinthians 6:19).

But there's another reason—ultimately even more impor-tant—that Junior has vigilantly watched over Richard. Junior needs Richard's help just as much as Richard needs Junior's help. This inter-dependency is explained in the scriptures. Let's start with Malachi in the Old Testament. Significantly, the last verse of the last chapter of the last book in the Old Testament (certainly a location of impor-tance) declares this essential message: "And he [the prophet Elijah] shall turn the heart of the fathers to the children, and the heart of the children to their fathers, lest I come and smite the earth with a curse" (Malachi 4:6).

This verse makes it clear that family relationships are vital. But why? For what purpose? And what exactly does it mean to turn the hearts of fathers (and mothers) to their children, and vice versa?

We can gain more insight by turning to Doctrine and Covenants 128:18. In this verse, the prophet Joseph Smith explains the meaning of Malachi 4:6, stating the following:

> The earth will be smitten with a curse unless there is a welding link of some kind or other between the fathers and the children, upon some subject or other. . . . For we without them cannot be made perfect; neither can they without us be made perfect. Neither can they nor we be made perfect without those who have died in the gospel also; for it is necessary in the ushering in of the dispensation of the fulness of times, which dispensation is now beginning to usher in,

that a whole and complete and perfect union, and welding together
of dispensations, and keys, and powers, and glories should take place,
and be revealed from the days of Adam even to the present time.

From this verse, we know that turning the hearts of fathers and
children to each other involves linking, or connecting, them. This
process allows them to obtain perfection. And how do we link the
generations? Joseph Smith answered this question in verse 18: "It is
the baptism for the dead." It is also through completing other temple
ordinances[11] for the dead, culminating in sealing parents to their children, through which parents and children are eternally connected (see
D&C 138:48). Only through sealing parents and children can we
avoid the curse warned of in Malachi 4.

Indeed, our very lives in heaven depend upon whether we heed
Malachi's warning. Joseph Smith cautioned, "My dearly beloved
brethren and sisters, let me assure you that these are principles in
relation to the dead and the living that cannot be lightly passed over,
as pertaining to our salvation. For their salvation is necessary and
essential to our salvation, as Paul says concerning the fathers—that
they without us cannot be made perfect—neither can we without our
dead be made perfect" (D&C 128:5).

I believe this fact is typically more clear and pressing for those
already living in heaven. Perhaps one reason is that they must rely
on us for help. Because they are no longer mortal, they can't complete essential ordinances for themselves; we must complete the work
for them.

For that reason, Junior has had a great interest in watching
over Richard, hoping that one day Richard would not only complete these ordinances for himself but would also complete them for
Junior and other family members. Only in this way can Junior be
made perfect; be linked to his parents, wife, and children; and live
with them eternally. And everyone in heaven wants to spend eternity with those they love. This desire and the need for Richard's help
are the reasons Junior protected his son. It's why Junior appeared to
me after my surgery. His goal was to let us know that families can
be linked together in heaven.

Doesn't it make sense that God would send our family members to teach us that we can be together with them again? Who are we more likely to believe than relatives whom we love? Moroni 7:22 declares: "For behold, God knowing all things, being from everlasting to everlasting, behold, he sent angels to minister unto the children of men, to make manifest concerning the coming of Christ; and in Christ there should come every good thing."

During that first dream, when Junior told me families can be together forever, I wasn't sure what he meant.[12] The concept was foreign to me. But at the same time, the idea was thrilling. I could be with Richard forever? How?

While I wanted to know, I wasn't ready for the answer yet. Just as Junior knew I wasn't ready to immediately see more than a sliver of heaven, he knew I wasn't ready to learn how to weld together an eternal family. But slowly, the answer came . . .

NOTES

1. Joseph F. Smith said, "Our deceased loved ones are greatly concerned about our well-being and happiness and can be appointed, when there is need, to bring messages of warning, reproof, or instruction to us" (*Gospel Doctrine*, 5th ed. [1939], 436). President Ezra Taft Benson stated, "The spirit world is not far away. Sometimes the veil between this life and the life beyond becomes very thin. Our loved ones who have passed on are not far from us" ("Life Is Eternal," *Ensign*, June 1971, 33).

2. Joseph F. Smith, *Gospel Doctrine*, 436.

3. *Discourses of Brigham Young*, 41.

4. See Genesis 16:7–8; 32:1; Judges 6:22; 1 Kings 19:5–7; Daniel 8:15–16; Zechariah 2: 3; and Luke 1:11–13, 26–27.

5. While angels are very aware of us, there's no need to feel like they're always eavesdropping or spying. They're actually quite busy (whether it be spending time with family, increasing their knowledge and abilities, or preaching the gospel), so they're not constantly watching what we're doing or invading our privacy.

6. I agree with Jeffrey R. Holland when he said that whether angels are "seen or unseen, they are always near" ("The Ministry of Angels," *Ensign,* November 2008).

7. *Journal of Discourses,* 3:368.

8. Joseph F. Smith, in Conference Report, April 1916.

9. Because our deceased relatives are near us and can often hear us, we need to make sure to always speak kindly of them.

10. While God is filled with all-encompassing love, He allows us to struggle at times, for our pains and inflictions are prime opportunities to become more like Him. Elder Richard G. Scott explained, "I am not suggesting that all of life's struggles will disappear as you do these things [pray, search the scripture, hold family night, and attend the temple]. We came to mortal life precisely to grow from trials and testing. Challenges help us become more like our Father in Heaven" ("Make the Exercise of Faith Your First Priority," *Ensign,* November 2014). Elder Jörg Klebingat said that when trials come, we should "try to force a smile, gaze heavenward, and say, 'I understand, Lord. I know what this is. A time to prove myself, isn't it?' Then partner with Him to endure well to the end" ("Approaching the Throne of God with Confidence," *Ensign,* November 2014).

11. Ordinances are sacred acts and ceremonies. They often involve making covenants, or promises, with Heavenly Father (The Guide to the Scriptures, s.v. "Ordinances," lds.org/scriptures/gs/ordinances). See chapter 8 for more discussion of ordinances.

12. I've since learned much about what it means. One critically important aspect is that we need to learn to love our family members while on earth—after all, we'll be with them for eternity! If the everlasting bond doesn't sound too appealing to you, decide how you can improve family relationships now in preparation for heaven. If you're feeling pretty happy about current family relationships, then it's time to go a step further by developing loving relationships with everyone else around you. From God's perspective, we're all related because we're His children. That means, as Richard's dad taught me, that everyone is family in heaven. I was thrilled the first time I saw Richard's parents visiting with my grandparents in heaven.

Chapter 6

CHRIST'S TRUE GOSPEL
IS ON EARTH TODAY

I watch a boy, maybe in his early teens, walk through a forest. Somehow, I know we're in New York. I look in the boy's eyes and see innocence yet wisdom beyond his years. I can tell he's deep in thought. What could be weighing on his mind so greatly?

I'm not sure who he is because I'm not accompanied by any of Richard's family members. Is the boy a relative? Something tells me he's not. Suddenly, I know his name is Joseph Smith, but I don't recall having ever heard that name before. I look for clues to uncover the mystery of who he is. His clothing suggests he's from an earlier era—maybe the early 1800s? I keep watching, wondering what will happen next.

The boy reaches a small clearing and stops. He looks in every direction, as if making sure he's alone. Then, taking a deep breath, he kneels on the ground and closes his eyes. After a moment, he starts praying aloud. But just as quickly, he stops. I can tell something is wrong, but I'm not sure what. He cries out for help. I feel his alarm, but I know there's nothing I can do. Suddenly, an intense light appears above him. I've seen this type of light before. It's the light of heaven. More specifically, it's the light that emanates from Jesus Christ.

Just as this thought crosses my mind, two images appear in the illumination. I recognize Jesus immediately. The other one points to Jesus and says, "This is My Beloved Son. Hear Him!"

My heart is pounding, not only because of seeing God the Father and Jesus Christ but also because of what I now know about the boy: he is destined to do something great.

But it wasn't until later that I learned just what he accomplished.

"I had another dream, Richard." A smile spread across his face. He obviously assumed I'd had another adventure with members of his family, and he loved hearing more about them.

"This one was a bit different. It was about the Mormons."

After I finished recounting the dream, Richard shook his head. "Jane, I'm not sure about this one. The Mormons are from Utah, not New York."

"Are you sure? My dream was in New York. I'm positive."

Biting his lip, Richard said, "Yes, I'm sure. I had a Mormon friend in high school, and he told the story of their first prophet. The church headquarters are somewhere in Utah."

We were both disconcerted. This was the first time any information in my dreams was incorrect. Or so we thought.

"Jane," Richard called to me. "I found something."

"What?" I asked, not knowing that what I was about to hear would have a prominent role in the next phase of my journey.

"You were right. About your dream. It did happen in New York."

My eyes widened in surprise. I felt so relieved, though I wasn't sure why. Did it really make a difference? We weren't members of the Mormon church, and I didn't think any of Richard's family members had been either. *Perhaps,* I thought, *I'm just glad that I hadn't misunderstood my dream.* After getting details right all the time, it had been unsettling to think that I'd been wrong about this dream.

Breaking me from my thoughts, Richard explained, "I looked up the details of the church and the prophet. It turns out that Joseph

Smith—that's the prophet's name—did have the vision in New York. He was fourteen years old."

Around the time of the dream, I started writing my first book. I felt impressed to add scripture references that supported what I saw in my dreams, but I couldn't always find Bible verses that quite fit. The Bible mentions angels but doesn't say anything about the angels being deceased family members.[1] I also looked for scriptures about my gift and eternal families. I found various scriptures about dreams, though they didn't mention visits from family members. And I didn't come up with any verses on families continuing in heaven. Why couldn't I find scriptural backing for my dreams of Richard's family and what they told me about eternal families? Everything else they had told me had been proven accurate. Surely the eternal nature of families had to be true too. I'd seen it for myself during my dreams.

I shared my feelings of confusion and discouragement with Richard.

"I'm certainly not a Bible scholar," I said. "Maybe I just don't understand the verses correctly."

"I don't know, honey." Richard shook his head. "I'm not any better with the scriptures than you are." His eyes got a faraway look, and I could tell that he was lost in thought.

I went back to writing, hoping that I might still find some scriptures.

"Jane, come here. I have something I want to show you."

I walked to the other room, where Richard was staring at the computer. "What are you reading?" I asked.

"I've been looking on the internet for information that matches what you've seen in your dreams."

I bit my lip. Although the dreams had been wonderful, sometimes I still wondered whether I was going crazy. How could I really be seeing Richard's parents? Was I somehow making everything up? With doubts running through my mind, I timidly asked, "So what did you find?"

"I found out about Joseph Smith, the boy you saw in the dream. The one where God and Christ appeared. He wrote something called the Book of Mormon. It's supposed to be like the Bible."

I grimaced as I returned Richard's gaze. I didn't know what to think. It seemed strange that someone had written a book like the Bible—and that I'd see him in a dream. "I've never heard of that book."

"I have, Jane. A friend gave me a Book of Mormon a long time ago, though I never read it and don't know what happened to it. I totally forgot about it until we started looking for scriptures that explained what you've learned in your dreams. When I searched on the internet, a lot of those things we couldn't find in the Bible, I found in the Book of Mormon."

Richard gestured to the computer screen. "See—look here. This is from the Book of Mormon."

I was still skeptical about the book, but I turned to the computer screen, which was filled with what looked like scripture verses. As I read, I couldn't help but think that they were beautiful. So I started to do a little research to find out more about the book. Who really wrote it? Was it really scripture? Did it support the Bible?

I was surprised how much I found from my brief internet search. Apparently, Joseph Smith was the author—or, as he described, the translator. How strange that I'd recently dreamed about him and now I was learning about his book. It had to be a coincidence, right? I didn't know how to make sense of it all, so I didn't give it much more thought. My main focus was on finishing my book.

But Richard wanted to learn more. As he read the Book of Mormon, he found verses about angels, dreams, and gifts of the Spirit. Here are just two examples referencing angels:[2]

- Moroni 7:22: For behold, God knowing all things, being from everlasting to everlasting, behold, he sent angels to minister unto the children of men, to make manifest concerning the coming of Christ; and in Christ there should come every good thing.

- Alma 32:23: And now, he [God] imparteth his word by angels unto men, yea, not only men but women also. Now this is not all; little children do have words given unto them many times, which confound the wise and the learned.

Richard and I were both excited to find something suggesting that what I was experiencing was possible. But I didn't know whether I should include the Book of Mormon references when writing my story—was the Book of Mormon really scripture?—so I left them out. I remained frustrated that I couldn't find Bible references to support all of my dreams, but I continued writing.

I'm not a natural-born writer, so the writing process was difficult. At times, I became so weary. But then I'd be reminded that God, who loved me so much, had asked me to write the book. It was the least I could do to thank Him for His kindness and mercy to me. On many occasions, Richard or I would get a feeling that a specific dream needed to be included in the book. We didn't know why, but the feeling was unmistakable, so I would write about the dream. God also helped me to remember the details of the dreams so I could describe them clearly. My understanding began to increase that when God asks you to do something, He helps you to accomplish it, just as promised in Philippians 4:13: "I can do all things through Christ which strengtheneth me."[3]

Finally, my book was finished. I had labored over it so long, trying to express everything I'd learned in my dreams: that God and Christ love us beyond comprehension, that heaven is a blissful place full of families. But though the book was finished, the hard work wasn't. Just as I'd felt strongly inspired to write down my experiences, I now felt an overwhelming need to make sure the message got to as many people as possible. To do that, I needed to go on a book tour—and a long one.

I had to be crazy. A book tour? I was still recovering from the trauma that my fall and subsequent surgery had exacted on my body. Richard owned a construction business and couldn't just up and leave to accompany me on a journey to who knows where. I wasn't aspiring to be a world-famous author; I was just trying to do what God had told me to do.

And for that very reason, I resolved to go on a book tour.

A book tour may not seem like a big thing to worry about—simply pick a few places where the book is likely to sell well (if you're lucky, they're by the beach), schedule a few events, and after two weeks on the road, you're back home. I knew the book tour that God had in mind for me was different. Richard and I felt impressed to focus on states in the South and Midwest. And a day or two in a few locations wasn't going to cut it. We weren't sure how long we'd stay on tour, but we knew it would be a while—long enough that I would quit my job and Richard would sell his business. We'd also need to sell most of our possessions; what remained would go in our RV, which would be our home for the months ahead.

At times, the uncertain journey before us was daunting. We loved California so much. It was our home, and we lived near my brother and sister-in-law. The thought of leaving made my heart break.

California or the Lord? California or the Lord? This question rushed through my mind frequently. But I already knew the answer. Richard and I had both prayed about it, asking for confirmation that what we were doing was the Lord's will. Each time we prayed, we felt a sweet feeling of peace and assurance. I understood that God was calling on me to share the message that He loves all people and that, because He loves us, He's made it possible for families to be together in heaven. I yearned to share this message, and I began to look forward to the tour with excitement.

Soon, we had everything loaded in the RV and waved goodbye to beautiful California, not knowing when—or, really, if—we'd return.

When we do what the Lord commands, He blesses us—far more than we ever expect. That's what I learned while on the book tour. The sadness of leaving behind our home, extended family, and friends was overshadowed by the amazing experiences God granted us during the book tour.

At least ten times, Richard and I were on the way to a book signing when the weather turned frightful. Perhaps the logical thing would have been to stop or turn around and wait out the storm. But I knew God wanted me to talk with the people who would be at the book signing. So I asked God to change the weather, if only long enough that we could make it to the signing in safety. Each time I asked, God lovingly answered my prayer. I learned that God will change the weather for ordinary people like me, not just for great people of God in biblical times (see Exodus 14:21; 1 Samuel 12:17–18; Matthew 8:24–26). If you ask with enough faith and it's not contrary to the Lord's plans, He will change the weather for you.

We held the book signings at a variety of locations, some not so typical for a promotional tour. But we went where God told us to, and that often included retirement homes. After I summarized the experiences in my book, members of the elderly audience would share their own beautiful angel stories.

One dear man told me his wife had died thirteen years before and he missed her beyond description. Every morning when he woke up, he could feel her by his side. "I've wondered whether she really is," the man said with a tremor in his voice. Tears started to run down my cheeks as he concluded, "Based on your story, I now believe she is. Thank you." I believe God guided me to retirement homes because the residents there tended to be open to my message. Often, they were already thinking about heaven. They realized their time in mortality was coming to an end, and they missed their spouses and other loved ones who had already gone to heaven.

However, the elderly weren't the only ones Richard and I felt inspired to meet with. We talked to people everywhere: bookstores, colleges, supermarkets, and even on the radio. The more I visited with others and they shared their stories, the more I realized that many people have been touched by angels. The problem is, most people don't have the spiritual knowledge to make sense of the experiences.[4] One young mother recounted that after her husband died, she repeatedly found coins in the cup holder of her car. She was mystified as to how they got there. Certainly, her two-year-old son wasn't behind the strange joke, but no one else was around when the money appeared. One day, as she found more change in the cup holder, she exclaimed, "Who on earth is doing this?"

"It's daddy," the little boy said. "He can get in the car."

The woman's heart skipped a beat. *Could it be him?*

But then she shook her head. *I'm being silly,* she told herself. *He's gone. There's no way he could leave me money.* She put aside the possibility, but she still wondered where the money was coming from.

Later, she heard me speaking on a radio station in her town. Her eyes grew wide as she listened to me share my stories. And then she knew. She still didn't understand exactly *how* her deceased husband was visiting her—or where he was getting the money—but she realized that somehow it was possible. Her husband loved her so much that he was leaving her a message: she wasn't alone and never would be.

Many people want to believe in angels. But it can be so hard to when we don't see them. We might be afraid of getting locked up in a mental hospital if we admit we believe in spiritual beings. I know what it's like to have people look at you funny when you describe your interactions with an angel—what some people would call a ghost. Nevertheless, I have to declare what I know to be true. Many of Richard's ancestors have visited me, and Richard and I have verified the accuracy of everything they've said. Rather than it being crazy to admit I've talked with angels, I'd be crazy to deny what I've experienced. So when people search my eyes and ask me whether angels are real, I answer them without hesitation: "Yes, I know they are. I've seen them!"

As clearly as I know my name is Jane, I know that angels exist, that they are always around us, and that they are helping us, even when we don't realize it.

When we receive a witness of the divine, we can become bold in declaring its reality to others—even those who aren't ready to believe. Though I wouldn't ever put myself on the same level as the great prophets, apostles, and disciples in the Bible, I do want to point out their confidence in testifying of that which they knew to be true. So let's look at a few examples, starting with Stephen, "a man full of faith and of the Holy Ghost." As he stood before an incensed group of Jews, he boldly described the vision before his eyes: "Behold, I see the heavens opened, and the Son of man standing on the right hand of God." He likely knew his words would further enrage the crowd, but he persisted. And for it, the Jews stoned him to death (see Acts 6:5; 7:55–60).

Paul serves as another awe-inspiring example. While imprisoned in Caesarea, Paul testified before King Agrippa and Festus (procurator of Judea) that the resurrected Christ appeared to Paul and commanded him to repent and then preach the gospel. Even after Festus exclaimed, "Paul, thou art beside thyself; much learning doth make thee mad," the prisoner remained firm in his words. Because Paul's declaration was so powerful, King Agrippa admitted, "Almost thou persuadest me to be a Christian" (see Acts 26).

The Bible contains many other examples of prophets and others who've boldly testified of Christ. While on the book tour I learned of another example, one that isn't in the Bible but that I'd glimpsed in my dream of the young man, though I didn't comprehend the meaning at the time. When I finally understood, it changed my life.

NOTES

1. See, for example, Luke 4:10; John 20:12; Hebrews 1:14; 13:2; and Revelation 14:6.
2. Here are a few more of the many Book of Mormon references to angels: 1 Nephi 11:30; 2 Nephi 4:24; Alma 13:24; Alma 19:34; Alma 36:5; Helaman 5:48; and Moroni 7:22. References to dreams include 1

Nephi 3:2; 1 Nephi 8:2; and Ether 9:3. Gifts of the spirit are mentioned in Alma 9:21 and Moroni 10:8–18.

3. For other examples of this promise, see Genesis 18:10–14 (the promise) and 21:1–2 (the fulfillment); 1 Kings 17: 10–16; 1 Nephi 3:7; 17:3, 50; and Doctrine and Covenants 5:34.

4. For some people, it's an issue of terminology. They may use the word *spirits* instead of *angels*. Or maybe they attribute the work of angels to the power of the universe.

Chapter 7

MY REBIRTH THROUGH BAPTISM

Hi Jane," she says. *Do I know her?* I ask myself. My eyes move from her blue ones to her curly blonde hair. She doesn't resemble anyone in Richard's family whom I've met. But she does look familiar. In fact, she looks a lot like my dad.

Before the question is fully formed in my mind, she answers it: "I'm Carol." I automatically feel a pain deep within. The reaction seems somewhat strange to me since Carol seems so happy, but all the previous times I've heard her name mentioned, it's been spoken with immense pain.

Carol is my aunt—my dad's sister—but this is the first time I've ever met her. She died while still in the womb. While that fact was hard enough for my family to bear, perhaps even more heart-rending was that, according to the religion I grew up in, because she hadn't had the opportunity to be baptized, her soul wouldn't be saved.

Yet here she is standing in front of me, so brilliant with light that she almost shimmers. She obviously had made it to heaven even without being baptized. This last thought wipes away the pain I felt just a moment before.

Carol gives me a big, warm hug, and I feel her intense love for me. "How is it that I've never met you before, but you seem to know me as well as a dear friend?"

"Oh, Jane, I've been watching over you since you were born," she says tenderly. "I've always looked out for you, making sure you stay out of harm's way—at least when it was God's will." I know she's thinking about my ankle—the one I shattered and that ultimately led to me seeing heaven. I'm no longer bitter about the accident. In fact, I praise God that this trial has allowed me to meet Richard's family—and, now, my family too.

I have so many questions for Carol, but something in her piercing eyes stops me. "Jane, I have a message for you. For you and our family—and everyone else too. It's *that* important."

I hold my breath. What's she going to say? I can't imagine it's anything bad, but behind the peace that Carol exudes, I sense a twinge of sadness. I clasp my hands in front of me and wait for her to explain.

She takes my hands in hers to reassure me. "It's okay, Jane. I have something wonderful to share with you."

I nod at her to go on. "I know everyone in the family has hurt so much . . . they thought I was consigned to hell because I wasn't baptized. But there's no need for the anguish—God saves little children in heaven, no matter whether they were baptized. They're innocent in His eyes."

A warmth rushes through me, confirming what she's said. And her words make sense based on everything I've learned about God, Jesus Christ, and heaven since I first met Junior. Yet the concept is so contrary to what I was taught to believe as a child—what my family still believes.

Knowing that I crave more information, Carol continues. "These children are being cared for in heaven by family members. Perhaps the most beautiful part of all is that they're waiting to greet their parents in heaven—there's a glorious reunion. They'll be able to live together as if they hadn't been separated in mortal life."

Tears fill Carol's beautiful, clear eyes. "I've seen so many mothers cry at losing their babies, thinking these precious gifts from God are lost forever. Jane, let them know the truth. Share my words of peace. God does require baptism, but not for the innocent little ones."

Soon after, Carol says it's time to leave. I know she's given me another piece of the puzzle, but I still have no idea what the overall picture is.

Sometime after the dream, I was chatting on the phone with my sister-in-law, Grace, who lived in California. We'd spent a lot of time together before I left for the book tour, and I missed being with her. But our conversation that day wasn't like any we'd previously had. Her excitement seemed almost tangible as she told me she'd just gotten baptized and confirmed in a new church.

"What?" I asked, my surprise almost as great as her excitement. "What church?"

"The Church of Jesus Christ of Latter-day Saints," Grace said. "But sometimes it's called the Mormon Church."

I suppose it seems strange, but at that time I didn't make the connection between the nickname of the Church and the Book of Mormon. I was somewhat curious about the book, but I was so busy trying to write *my* book and find scriptures to support what I was writing that I hadn't taken the time to learn more about the Book of Mormon. It hadn't occurred to me that the book belonged to a specific church.

I listened as Grace eagerly told me about her new religion. "Jane, this church teaches the same things you've experienced and learned in heaven!" My heart started beating faster. Was there really a church that taught what I'd learned? I'd come to doubt that during the book tour. Richard and I had visited numerous churches, and we'd repeatedly been told that we were misguided—or worse—for believing what I'd written in my book. The pastors told me that angels no longer visited the earth, particularly to speak with an average person like me. And families certainly wouldn't be together in heaven. According to the pastors, I was delusional. I might have started to believe it myself if Richard hadn't confirmed to me that I was sane and reminded me that everything I'd learned about his family in my dreams was accurate.

So I yearned for Grace to be right, for her church to believe what I knew to be true from personal experience. But I didn't want to get my hopes up too high. Grace obviously noticed my hesitancy. "Jane, I have a friend in Oskaloosa who's a member of the Church. You should go visit her. She can explain the Church's beliefs a lot better than I can."

I'd grown up in Oskaloosa, and Richard and I were visiting the town for the book tour, but I still wasn't sure about meeting with Grace's friend. At first, I made excuses. But I knew I needed to find out more about Grace's church. I reasoned with myself that meeting with her friend certainly couldn't be worse than the rejection I'd faced when talking with pastors from other faiths. So finally I agreed, and Richard and I arranged to meet Grace's friend.

That's why Richard and I found ourselves outside of a Latter-day Saint Church building in Oskaloosa one Friday. After I took one final deep breath, we walked in. My anxiety and uncertainty were immediately overcome by the sensations of light and happiness. Being there felt *right,* similar to how being with Richard's family in heaven felt right. A woman approached us, a smile beaming on her face. She introduced herself as Grace's friend and then gave us a tour of the Church building. We walked down the hall and stopped in front of a painting hung on the wall: a beautiful depiction of Jesus Christ. Looking at that picture, I felt His love just as I did when seeing Him in my dreams. After a time, we continued down the hall, taking in other paintings and basking in the light and love—and something else too. Richard and I weren't quite sure what it was, but it was making us cry. But these tears weren't the kind that come when you're sad or feel empty. We felt calm. Secure. Peaceful.

We eventually made our way back to the entrance. Before Richard and I left, our new friend invited us to come back on Sunday to attend worship services. I thanked her for the invitation, signed a copy of my book, and then handed it to her.

Taking the book, she smiled. "I have something for you too."

"Really, you don't need to give us anything," I protested.

"Oh, yes. Yes, I do." She gave me a copy of the Book of Mormon, as well as a book called *Gospel Principles.*

After thanking her for the books and promising to return on Sunday, Richard and I headed outside. Though I was reluctant to leave the peace I'd felt while in the church, I was also excited to look through the books I'd received. What would I find in them? Would they agree with what I'd learned in heaven?

While Richard went fishing, I decided to start reading *Gospel Principles*, the shorter of the two books I'd been given. I found that each chapter focused on a different Church belief, which I figured would make it pretty easy to learn more about this church—a church whose prophet I had dreamed about and which my sister-in-law now belonged to. I flipped to a chapter of interest and started reading.

I was blown away. My sister-in-law was right—the Church did support what I'd learned in my dreams: Jesus Christ loves everyone, God gives people spiritual gifts, and families can live together in heaven. I got out a highlighter and started marking everything in *Gospel Principles* that supported what was in my book. All the things I'd searched for in the Bible but couldn't find as I was writing my book—they were in *Gospel Principles*! My heart beating faster, I opened the Book of Mormon. What would I find?

As I turned the pages, tears slipped from my eyes. Why did things related to this church make me cry? But just as before, I wasn't weeping because of sorrow or pain. Quite the opposite—I felt wonderful. And so I continued reading.

I was impatient for Richard to return. I couldn't wait to tell him what I'd learned. And what I'd decided. So when he walked through the door, I couldn't help but blurt out my thoughts.

"We're joining the Church, Richard!"

His look of surprise and confusion was understandable, of course. I knew I needed to explain everything, but I was just too excited. And amazed. And somewhat shocked myself. All I could say was, "I know it's right. That feeling—the one that's been making me cry—it's from God. I want that feeling all the time, and the Mormon Church is the key."

I started telling Richard about everything I'd learned from *Gospel Principles*. I showed him example after example of how the information matched my dreams. Richard was quiet, but I could tell he was feeling the same way as I was. We couldn't wait to go to the Church services on Sunday.

As we entered the Church building two days later, we again experienced that indescribable feeling and we started to cry. We cried the whole time. It wasn't just because of what we heard during the sermon; it was also because of what we saw: the adoring way husbands looked at wives, the kindness siblings showed to each other. There was no way not to notice the love emanating from everyone. When the services were over, we slowly walked to the door, tears flowing down our faces. (It was becoming quite the habit.) We knew we needed to learn more about the Church.

But before we could, I had a feeling we should leave Oskaloosa because a terrible snowstorm was brewing. The only way to avoid the heavy ice and snow that could destroy our motorhome was to head south. Fast! We prayed as we made our way through Iowa, Missouri, and finally Arkansas. The weather was so bad that we had to stop in Little Rock. Richard and I were safe and happy to have escaped the blinding blizzard that had hit Oskaloosa. By then, we'd learned to trust my feelings, so we didn't waste time getting on the road. Soon after arriving in Little Rock, we saw a chapel for The Church of Jesus Christ of Latter-day Saints. A voice told me we needed to go inside, but I was nervous. I wanted what the Church members had; I wanted to keep feeling the way I had when at the church in Oskaloosa. But I didn't even know what was required to be a member of the Church.

"Please, God," I prayed, "let the Church accept us." As I repeated the words over and over in my mind, Richard and I timidly walked in. We found what appeared to be the main meeting room and attempted to just slip into the back to avoid drawing attention to ourselves. However, that was hard to do, considering everyone in the room was wearing their Sunday best, while I was wearing a pantsuit and Richard was in a red jogging outfit. Before we could hide, a woman cheerfully approached us. (It seemed that all Church members were perpetually happy!)

"Hi! Are you new?" she asked, as if it weren't obvious.

Deciding to be completely honest, I told her, "Yes. And we want to be baptized!"

After she recovered from a moment of shock, her smile became even larger, which I hadn't thought possible. "Wonderful! Have you talked to the missionaries?"

"Um, no. Do we need to?"

She was already leading us to the other side of the room, where we saw two young men wearing suits with name tags on the pocket. Somehow, these "elders," as the kind lady called them, seemed even more joyful than she did. I could barely keep myself from asking why everyone was so, so happy. Was that a requirement to join the Church? No, I didn't think so. I somehow knew that being happy came from being in the Church. That was one of the reasons I wanted to be a member.

As we talked with the missionaries, Richard and I learned that my earlier fear of not being allowed into the Church was unnecessary. Elder Whelan and Elder McMurtrey told us that after they taught us lessons about the basic principles of the Church and we agreed to keep God's commandments, we could be baptized. Now it was hard to decide who was more ecstatic—the missionaries or Richard and me!

We met with the missionaries several times for gospel lessons—about Joseph Smith's vision of God and Jesus Christ (which I knew about because of my dream), about Jesus Christ and His Atonement, about repentance, and about the need to be obedient to the commandments. Each time we talked with the missionaries, we felt that special, indescribable feeling, and we didn't want them to leave. We soaked up what they said. When they bore their testimonies of Christ and His gospel, it was as if a big spotlight were shining from them, similar to the light that radiated from everything in heaven. And speaking of heaven, everything the missionaries taught us agreed with what I'd learned in my dreams. I knew what I was hearing was right. How else could it have matched my dreams?

While what I had seen in heaven matched, the missionaries filled in a lot of the gaps in what I'd learned from visiting with Richard's family in heaven. We learned that there had been an apostasy in Christ's Church after His Apostles died (many through martyrdom). Without Apostles on the earth, priesthood authority was lost, and the doctrines of the Church became corrupted in the following decades and centuries. Knowledge about essential principles—such as that the members of the Godhead are separate beings—was lost. This loss of knowledge led to the spiritual dark ages, as the Bible prophesied would happen (see, for example, Isaiah 60:2; Amos 8:11–12; 2 Thessalonians 2:3). Yet many people still searched for spiritual truth and guidance, which led to the Reformation during the 1500s to mid-1600s and to the establishment of many churches.

Just as God had told biblical prophets that an apostasy would come, He also promised that He would establish His Church once again upon the earth (see 2 Thessalonians 2:1–3; Isaiah 29:13–14; Acts 3:19–21). That time came in the early 1800s through Joseph Smith. In the spring of 1820, at the age of fourteen, he felt a great desire to join one of the many churches in the area where he lived in upstate New York. But he was confused about which one was correct—he didn't want to join just any church; he wanted to join God's Church. Perplexed, he turned to the scriptures (an intelligent boy!). As he read, he was greatly inspired by James 1:5—"If any of you lack wisdom, let him ask of God, that giveth to all men liberally, and upbraideth not; and it shall be given him." He believed these words and decided to ask God which church to join. Wanting some privacy, he walked to a grove of trees near his home. Kneeling, he began to pray aloud to God.

Then commenced a series of events Joseph never expected. "I was seized upon by some power which entirely overcame me. . . . Thick darkness gathered around me, and it seemed to me for a time as if I were doomed to sudden destruction" (Joseph Smith—History 1:15). This is an important lesson for us all. When we pray with real desire, Satan doesn't like it, and he will try to stop us, as he tried to stop

Joseph. Fortunately, we probably won't ever experience so forceful a situation as Joseph did. So why did Satan hit so hard on a fourteen-year-old boy? Because Joseph was about to commune with God—face-to-face. As Joseph later recounted, "Exerting all my powers to call upon God to deliver me out of the power of this enemy which had seized upon me . . . I saw a pillar of light exactly over my head, above the brightness of the sun, which descended gradually until it fell upon me. It no sooner appeared than I found myself delivered from the enemy which held me bound. When the light rested upon me I saw two Personages, whose brightness and glory defy all description, standing above me in the air. One of them spake unto me, calling me by name and said, pointing to the other—This is My Beloved Son. Hear Him!" (Joseph Smith—History 1:16–17).

The Son—Jesus Christ—then answered Joseph's question: He shouldn't join any of the churches he'd considered because they "were all wrong." Although they contained pieces of the gospel, each was missing essential principles and also included erroneous teachings, which is understandable considering the long apostasy.[1] God and Jesus Christ were ready to once again establish their gospel in its purity on the earth. But this vision to Joseph Smith was just the beginning. He had much to learn and do before Christ's Church could once again be introduced.

In the following ten years, Joseph Smith was visited by angels: Moroni told Joseph where to find gold plates containing the Book of Mormon; John the Baptist conferred the Aaronic Priesthood on Joseph; and the Apostles Peter, James, and John conferred the Melchizedek Priesthood on Joseph (see Joseph Smith—History 1:30–47, 68–72; D&C 27:12). He translated the gold plates (which were written in what the book calls reformed Egyptian), published the translation as the Book of Mormon, and received many revelations before the divinely appointed date of April 6, 1830—the day Heavenly Father's Church was formally established on the earth once again. That church is called The Church of Jesus Christ of Latter-day Saints. For Joseph's important role in the restoration of God's Church, members of the Church revere him, but they don't worship him.

We also learned that Heavenly Father has a plan for all of His children. That plan started before we came to earth and extends through our lives here and into our lives in heaven. His goal is for us to live with Him once again, so He can give us all He has—making us "joint-heirs with Christ" (Romans 8:17). For us to obtain that glory, we need to have agency and then use that agency to make good choices, including keeping God's commandments. Of course, no matter how hard we try, we won't be perfect. If you're like me, you're prone to imperfection every day. Sure, most people aren't committing huge sins, like murdering or committing adultery, but even the small ones, like telling "white lies" or yelling at family members, are a problem because Jesus said that we need to be perfect (see Matthew 5:48) and that He "cannot look upon sin with the least degree of allowance" (Alma 45:16; D&C 1:31). That puts us in a tough spot, doesn't it?

That's where Christ's Atonement comes in. He is the *only* way we could possibly live with Him and Heavenly Father again. Through His Atonement and Resurrection, we'll not only live again but we can be made clean so that we can dwell eternally in heaven. However, for us to get there we must repent. We show our desire to repent and be made clean by agreeing to be baptized. And then after that, we need to repent whenever we make a mistake. For me, that means repenting not just monthly or weekly but every day. Maybe I was impatient with someone or didn't follow a prompting from the Holy Ghost to serve someone. Sure, those aren't big things, but even they need to be repented of if we want to be completely clean. Don't delay repentance. Not only will repenting bring you peace but it will also mean that you're prepared to meet God whenever He decides it's your time.

The missionaries also taught us that before being baptized, Richard and I needed to be married. We loved each other dearly but hadn't bothered with getting married because we saw it as just a formality. A marriage certificate was just a piece of paper. But we started to think otherwise the first time we attended Latter-day Saint worship services. The love we saw among husbands and wives was so touching that Richard had turned to me and said, "Maybe we should get a marriage license." I was surprised, but I was feeling the same way.

And that's why on January 31, 2013, Richard and I stood hand in hand before the bishop and made our wedding vows. Though the ceremony was simple, without the usual pomp and circumstance, I couldn't have been happier. It seemed that my love for Richard was even stronger than before. We were also both touched by the genuine love that Church members showed for us that day. Though they hardly knew us, several came to the wedding to demonstrate their support. That was the first of many ways in which Church members taught us that being part of the Church meant being part of a family. It made me think of Christ's abundant love for everyone, which I repeatedly saw in my dreams. Richard and I could hardly wait to become official members of the Church by being baptized.

Elder Whelan turned to me, a smile of pure joy on his face. "Are you ready?"

I returned the smile, but I knew my nervousness was evident. Taking a deep breath, I responded, "Yes." It was February 2, 2013, and I'd just watched Richard be baptized. Now, it was my turn. I locked gazes with Richard, whose hair was still wet. He looked happier than I'd ever seen him before. I looked into the faces of the Church members who'd come to support and celebrate with Richard and me. In a few minutes, I would be a member of this amazing Church family—Christ's family.

The thought was thrilling, but being baptized represented a huge turning point in my life. As I walked down the steps into the baptismal font, questions raced through my mind. Was I really worthy to enter God's Church? I certainly hadn't done anything horrible in my life, but more than ever before I was painfully aware of my imperfections. I remembered the promise in the Book of Mormon: by being baptized, God would forgive *all* my sins (see Mosiah 26:22; Alma 7:14; and D&C 58:42). But how could He?

I reached Elder Whelan in the baptismal font, and he took my hand. In that moment, it was like an electric jolt ran through me. Although I still didn't understand *how* God could forgive all my sins,

I knew that He *would* forgive them. And that's really all that mattered. I was ready.

In a clear, strong voice, Elder Whelan spoke the words of the baptismal ordinance and then submerged me in the water. As the water engulfed me, my entire life flashed before my eyes. The things I cherished, the things I regretted. I saw them all. And then just as quickly, my head was back out of the water, and I was *clean*. I felt a brilliant white light and an overwhelming feeling of love encompassing me. Later, Richard said that I was glowing. I knew it was God's way of telling me He was pleased with my decision to enter His Church. I was reborn, beginning a glorious new life—one that was focused on God and Jesus Christ—just as Jesus had said was necessary (see John 3:3–5).

It all seemed almost too good to be true. But this time, I was quite sure I wasn't dreaming. I was wide awake—and couldn't have been happier.

In the following days, I couldn't get enough of the gospel. I loved reading the scriptures and learning more about God's plan for His children. If I had a question, all I needed to do was read the scriptures, particularly the Book of Mormon, and I'd find the answer. It was almost as if God had put the answer there just for me. Time and again, I was delighted to learn about another gospel principle that supported what I'd learned in my visits with Richard's family. Every day I was fitting together more of the pieces, and every day I was cultivating a stronger conviction that the gospel is perfect, just as God is perfect.

Delving into the scriptures was a new experience for Richard and me. Both of us had associated with particular religions growing up, but neither one of us was familiar with the scriptures. We thought the Bible was hard to understand, so we didn't read it. And the stories it contained were just that—stories, not real accounts of real people. It seemed so hard to relate to the people in the Bible, but after joining the Church and interacting with Richard's family in heaven, I had an epiphany. The people in the Bible are like ancestors![2] Now when I read the scriptures, I think of the protagonists as my grandparents, aunts, uncles, parents, siblings, and children. Even though I never met Richard's father during his life, I know he was mortal just like me. The same is true about everyone in the scriptures; they were real people with real challenges. With that perspective, I try to understand them and their experiences more, even when the scriptural language is hard for me to understand. In fact, it's thrilling. (What kid hasn't wanted to read through a sister's diary? Reading the scriptures can give us the same inside look at ancestors in the ancient world.)

Knowing that the people I'm reading about are relatives makes their stories more powerful. That's why reading the New Testament after I was baptized was such a moving experience for me. When I read that John the Baptist was beheaded, I cried as I would have at the death of someone I knew personally. And when I reached the description of Christ's Atonement and crucifixion, I felt as if my heart were torn apart. He bled from every pore for *me*. He allowed the Jews to kill Him because He loves *me*. Though I can't fathom the depths of His love, reading about and pondering His sacrifice brings me to my knees in humility.

When I finished the New Testament, I cried again—I didn't want it to be over! I wanted to read more about my ancestors and the revelations they received from God. Well, guess what I realized? The family narratives and revelations don't end with the New Testament. Through Joseph Smith, we've received many other books of scripture: the Book of Mormon, Doctrine and Covenants, and Pearl of Great Price. In thinking about it all, more than once I've shouted out, *Thank you, God!*

I love reading about Grandpa Nephi building a ship and Uncle Moroni raising the Title of Liberty. I'm so proud of what my ancestors did! I have a feeling that when we reach heaven, we'll be glad that we became familiar with the people in the scriptures. We'll be meeting them there, and we'll feel pretty sheepish if we don't know that Esther saved the Jews from genocide or that Helaman led the two thousand stripling warriors (see Esther 3–7 and Alma 53).

Reading the Book of Mormon has increased my understanding of the Bible because the Book of Mormon clarifies and expands on many of the principles presented in the Bible. I'll share just a few examples. In Luke 22:41–44, we read of Jesus atoning for us in the Garden of Gethsemane:

> And he was withdrawn from them [His Apostles] about a stone's cast, and kneeled down, and prayed,
>
> Saying, Father, if thou be willing, remove this cup from me: nevertheless not my will, but thine, be done.
>
> And there appeared an angel unto him from heaven, strengthening him.
>
> And being in an agony he prayed more earnestly: and his sweat was as it were great drops of blood falling down to the ground.

Some people have interpreted "his sweat was as it were great drops of blood" to mean that Jesus didn't bleed but rather that he sweat profusely. That interpretation greatly minimizes the suffering Jesus experienced, perhaps even suggesting that He didn't really atone for humankind. But the Book of Mormon verifies that our Savior did indeed bleed—from every pore—to atone for our sins. Mosiah 3:7 tells us, "He shall suffer temptations, and pain of body, hunger, thirst, and fatigue, even more than man can suffer, except it be unto death; for behold, *blood cometh from every pore*, so great shall be his anguish for the wickedness and the abominations of his people" (emphasis added).

The Book of Mormon has also helped me understand the principle of grace. In the Bible, Paul taught the Ephesians that "by grace are ye saved through faith; and that not of yourselves: it is the gift of God" (Ephesians 2:8). Based on that scripture, it could be argued that if we believe, we'll be saved regardless of how we act. Thankfully, verses in the Book of Mormon provide a more complete explanation of how grace works. Nephi stated the conditions plainly when he wrote, "We know that it is by grace that we are saved, after all we can do" (2 Nephi 25:23). And what is "all we can do"? Moroni 10:32 provides an answer: "If ye shall deny yourselves of all ungodliness, and love God with all your might, mind and strength, then is his grace sufficient for you, that by his grace ye may be perfect in

Christ." Only as we do these things and repent when we stumble will we be recipients of God's matchless grace: "After ye are reconciled unto God, . . . it is only in and through the grace of God that ye are saved" (2 Nephi 10:24).

Another vital clarification that comes through the Book of Mormon concerns whether little children need to be baptized. The Old Testament doesn't mention baptism, but the New Testament establishes that this sacred ordinance is important to God. That's why Jesus Christ set the example by being baptized, even though He had no sins to be cleansed of. Jesus later declared, "Except a man be born of water and of the Spirit, he cannot enter into the kingdom of God" (John 3:5). But what of children like my aunt Carol, who die before they have the opportunity to be baptized? Many people have interpreted Jesus's declaration to mean that anyone of any age who isn't baptized will be locked out of heaven. Luckily, the Book of Mormon clarifies: "It is solemn mockery before God, that ye should baptize little children. . . . Awful is the wickedness to suppose that God saveth one child because of baptism, and the other must perish because he hath no baptism" (Moroni 8:9, 15). Moroni also explained why this false principle is so grievous to God: "Listen to the words of Christ, your Redeemer, your Lord and your God. Behold, I came into the world not to call the righteous but sinners to repentance; the whole need no physician, but they that are sick; wherefore, little children are whole, for they are not capable of committing sin; wherefore the curse of Adam is taken from them in me, that it hath no power over them" (Moroni 8:8).[3]

These examples highlight one of the reasons we need the Book of Mormon in addition to the Bible. Of course, a lot of people argue that the Bible is complete and that any additional scriptures can't be from God. Our wise, all-knowing Heavenly Father knew that people would make that argument, and He addressed it in the Book of Mormon. He told Nephi that in our day, when He had once more established His Church on the earth:

> Many of the Gentiles[4] shall say: A Bible! A Bible! We have got a Bible, and there cannot be any more Bible. . . .
>
> Know ye not that there are more nations than one? Know ye

not that I, the Lord your God, have created all men, and that I
remember those who are upon the isles of the sea; and that I rule
in the heavens above and in the earth beneath; and I bring forth
my word unto the children of men, yea, even upon all the nations
of the earth?

Wherefore murmur ye, because that ye shall receive more
of my word? Know ye not that the testimony of two nations is a
witness unto you that I am God, that I remember one nation like
unto another? Wherefore, I speak the same words unto one nation
like unto another. And when the two nations shall run together the
testimony of the two nations shall run together also.

And I do this that I may prove unto many that I am the same
yesterday, today, and forever; and that I speak forth my words
according to mine own pleasure. And because that I have spoken
one word ye need not suppose that I cannot speak another; for my
work is not yet finished; neither shall it be until the end of man,
neither from that time henceforth and forever.

Wherefore, because that ye have a Bible ye need not suppose
that it contains all my words; neither need ye suppose that I have
not caused more to be written. . . .

For behold, I shall speak unto the Jews and they shall write it;
and I shall also speak unto the Nephites and they shall write it; and
I shall also speak unto the other tribes of the house of Israel, which
I have led away, and they shall write it; and I shall also speak unto
all nations of the earth and they shall write it.[5]

And it shall come to pass that the Jews shall have the words of
the Nephites, and the Nephites shall have the words of the Jews;
and the Nephites and the Jews shall have the words of the lost
tribes of Israel; and the lost tribes of Israel shall have the words of
the Nephites and the Jews. (2 Nephi 29:3–5, 7–10, 12–13)

Don't you agree that the power and truths in these verses are thrilling? They also make perfect sense. Since God is the Father of all mortals, why would He limit His communication to those in one area of
the world? Heavenly Father isn't a "respecter of persons," meaning He
speaks to all His children and that He won't withhold His gospel or
salvation from any group of people (see Acts 10:34; D&C 1:35; 38:16).[6]
Therefore, He has provided different groups with different books of
scripture. And in these modern days, the different sets of scriptures[7]

have been brought together so that we might benefit more fully. The Bible talks about the coming forth and bringing together of these complementary sets of scriptures: "Moreover, thou son of man, take thee one stick, and write upon it, For Judah, and for the children of Israel his companions: then take another stick, and write upon it, For Joseph, the stick of Ephraim, and for all the house of Israel his companions: And join them one to another into one stick; and they shall become one in thine hand" (Ezekiel 37:16–17). The stick of Judah represents the Bible, while the stick of Ephraim represents the Book of Mormon, which was written largely by descendants of Ephraim.[8]

Now, even with an understanding that God has given us more than just the Bible, some people might feel overwhelmed with the resulting heavy load of reading. If you count all the pages in the King James Bible, Book of Mormon, Doctrine and Covenants, and Pearl of Great Price, that's 2,476 pages (not including introductory pages). Yowza! Yeah, that's a lot to read. But they're the most interesting and life-changing pages you'll ever lay eyes on. Plus, no one ever said you have to read through all of it every year. You've got a whole lifetime to study, so set a pattern of reading some each day. If you haven't already established a daily reading habit or haven't developed a testimony of the scriptures, please make it a priority to do so. Don't wait until New Year's—we all know those resolutions never stick anyway, right? Start tomorrow. Actually, don't even wait until tomorrow. Put my book down, and open the scriptures! (How many authors tell you to stop reading their book and start reading a different book instead? That shows you how serious I am about the need to read the scriptures.) I completely agree with President Howard W. Hunter's words: "Where could there be more profitable use of time than reading from the scriptural library the literature that teaches us to know God and understand our relationship to him? Time is always precious to busy people, and we are robbed of its worth when hours are wasted in reading or viewing that which is frivolous and of little value."[9] While I certainly hope my book isn't frivolous or lacking in value, if reading my book is keeping you from reading the scriptures, then I sincerely hope you'll put my book down.

Why am I so insistent about reading the scriptures? Well, I've developed a testimony of them. That they speak the truth—even God's word. That they give me answers to a wide range of questions. That they help me feel happy, peaceful, and grateful. That they teach me what to do to live with Heavenly Father and Jesus Christ in heaven. If my simple testimony isn't enough to convince you, then let's take a look at what some spiritual giants—including prophets of God—have said.

Let's start with the Apostle Robert D. Hales, who said that "when we want to speak to God, we pray. And when we want Him to speak to us, we search the scriptures; for His words are spoken through His prophets."[10] Another apostle, Richard G. Scott, explained: "Scriptures are like packets of light that illuminate our minds and give place to guidance and inspiration from on high. They can become the key to open the channel to communion with our Father in Heaven and His Beloved Son, Jesus Christ." Elder Scott also said that scripture verses, particularly those we've memorized, can become unfaltering friends—the kind you can call day or night and they'll come to your rescue. But there's more. The "scriptures can calm an agitated soul, giving peace, hope, and a restoration of confidence in one's ability to overcome the challenges of life. They have potent power to heal emotional challenges when there is faith in the Savior. They can accelerate physical healing."[11]

God inspired scripture writers to include the very information that He knew we would need. But what if you have a unique circumstance that you don't think is addressed in the scriptures? I challenge you to pray for the Holy Ghost's guidance and then read the scriptures; with the combination of prayer, the Spirit, and the scriptures, I think you'll find your answer. Now, I'm not saying you'll find the answer word for word in a verse you read, but as you search the scriptures and seek guidance, the Holy Ghost will help you know how the information you're reading applies. Or, He might whisper unrelated words to you, but they'll come because you showed faith by turning to the scriptures for an answer. Elder Hales promised that as we read the scriptures and "listen to the promptings of the Holy Spirit," God will teach us. This wise Apostle of God then cautioned: "If you have not heard His voice speaking to you lately, return with new eyes and new ears to the scriptures. They are our spiritual lifeline."[12]

In particular, we should read from the Book of Mormon—daily. Why prioritize this book over the other scriptures God has given us? There are a lot of reasons, actually. Enough to fill up a book on its own. So I'm only going to summarize a few of the ones that stand out the most to me. First, the Book of Mormon was written for our day. It wasn't composed for the people who lived at the time it was being written; they didn't have access to it.[13] The first time it became available to anyone besides those who wrote in it was after Joseph Smith translated it in 1829 and then published in 1830.

The ancient authors of the Book of Mormon knew it was meant for our day. The prophet Mormon declared, "Behold, I speak unto you as if ye were present, and yet ye are not. But behold, Jesus Christ hath shown you unto me, and I know your doing" (Mormon 8:35). Nephi concluded his writings in the Book of Mormon by stating, "And now, my beloved brethren, all those who are of the house of Israel, and all ye ends of the earth, I speak unto you as the voice of one crying from the dust [i.e., someone who died long ago]: Farewell until that great day shall come" (2 Nephi 33:13). Moroni, the last to write in the Book of Mormon, similarly testified, "The time speedily cometh that ye shall know that I lie not, for ye shall see me at the bar of God; and the Lord God will say unto you: Did I not declare my words unto you, which were written by this man, like as one crying from the dead, yea, even as one speaking out of the dust?" (Moroni 10:27).

Because the Book of Mormon was written for our day, the information it contains is pertinent to us.[14] Many times, the authors of the book admitted that they didn't know why they were inspired to write specific things or to preserve certain writings, except that they knew it was "for a wise purpose."[15] I love Mormon's description: "I shall take these plates, which contain these prophesyings and revelations, and put them with the remainder of my record, for they are choice unto me; and I know they will be choice unto my brethren. And I do this for a wise purpose; for thus it whispereth me, according to the workings of the Spirit of the Lord which is in me. And now, I do not know all things; but the Lord knoweth all things which are to come;

wherefore, he worketh in me to do according to his will" (Words of Mormon 1:7). That "wise purpose" was so we could have "the prophesyings and revelations" that were "choice unto" Mormon.

Ready for the next reason we should read from the Book of Mormon every day? Let's turn to none other than Joseph Smith, who certainly was qualified to speak about the Book of Mormon. He boldly (and truthfully) declared, "The Book of Mormon [is] the most correct of any book on earth, and the keystone of our religion, and a man [will] get nearer to God by abiding by its precepts, than by any other book" (Introduction to the Book of Mormon).[16] Basically, if you want to become closer to God, then reading the Book of Mormon is *the* go-to strategy. One reason that the Book of Mormon is so powerful and correct, the very keystone of the LDS religion, is that "unlike the Bible, which passed through generations of copyists, translators, and corrupt religionists who tampered with the text, the Book of Mormon came from writer to reader in just one inspired step of translation," accomplished by Joseph Smith, with God's help. Therefore, the Book of Mormon's testimony of Jesus Christ is clear and undiluted.[17]

After seeing Jesus in my dreams and feeling His love, then learning about and being baptized into His Church, there is nothing I want more than to draw nearer to God, to become more like Him, and to feel His presence in my daily life. I am *so* grateful that reading the Book of Mormon allows me to do those exact things.[18]

Ezra Taft Benson, the thirteenth prophet and President of The Church of Jesus Christ of Latter-day Saints, described the power that comes from studying the Book of Mormon: "You will find greater power to resist temptation. You will find the power to avoid deception. You will find the power to stay on the strait and narrow path." And that is one of the reasons reading the scriptures draws us closer to Heavenly Father. President Benson identified a further reason to read from the Book of Mormon: "When you begin to hunger and thirst after those words, you will find life in greater and greater abundance."[19] To me, that means that we'll feel happier, more peaceful, and more satisfied with our lives. I know that's been the case for me.

Even if you believe that these blessings will come from reading the Book of Mormon—and other scriptures—I realize that scripture study may still appear to be a daunting task (and hence one you never get to). Start by reading just five minutes a day. Once you've gotten into the habit, bump up the time to ten minutes. Pretty soon, you might find that you've forgotten to stop reading after ten minutes and have gone for fifteen minutes or more. Maybe you'll be so engrossed in your ancestors' stories or will be feeling the Spirit so strongly that you won't want to stop. You may be skeptical, but if you read with the true intent to learn, it will happen.

If you're struggling to establish a consistent scripture-reading habit, think about the time of day you're reading. I like to read in the morning for several reasons. For one, it sets the tone for the whole day. During the day, I'll find myself thinking about what I read and even getting new insights. In a way, it extends my scripture study past the time I actually spend reading. It also provides direction for my day, helping me focus on God and Jesus Christ, as well as following their example of good works. I've experienced what President Henry B. Eyring described: "A morning prayer and an early search in the scriptures to know what we should do for the Lord can set the course of a day. We can know which task, of all those we might choose, matters most to God and therefore to us."[20] I also read my scriptures in the morning because then I know I'm sure to get it done every day. If you're like me, the day gets busier, more unpredictable, and therefore crazier with each hour of the day. By the evening, many of the things I was planning to do have been preempted by little emergencies, requests to help others, and other surprises. Next thing I know, I'm ready to fall into bed, hoping to get a little sleep before starting another eventful day. For me at least, if I waited until nighttime to read the scriptures, I'd either end up cutting my study time short or would get little out of what I was reading because my brain was shutting off for the night—if I could even stay awake. I firmly believe that the most important things need to be completed first, and so scripture study is the first thing I do each day.

Leaders of The Church of Jesus Christ of Latter-day Saints have noted spiritual benefits of waking up early in the morning. During Harold B. Lee's service as an apostle (he later became the eleventh President of The Church of Jesus Christ of Latter-day Saints), he provided the following counsel to Marion G. Romney, who had just been called as an assistant to the Quorum of the Twelve Apostles: "Go to bed early and get up early. If you do, your body and mind will become rested and then, in the quiet of those early morning hours, you will receive more flashes of inspiration and insight than at any other time of the day." Romney later said, "From that day on, I put that counsel into practice, and I know it works."[21] Boyd K. Packer similarly noted that when under pressure, "I'd be early to bed and getting up in the wee hours of the morning, when I could be close to Him who guides this work."[22] Though these quotes don't mention scripture study, I think it's reasonable to assume that during those "wee hours," these Church leaders were praying, reading the scriptures, and meditating, which helped facilitate the "flashes of inspiration and insight."[23]

All that being said, maybe early-morning scripture study just doesn't work for you. Hey, that's okay. What really matters is that you figure out when the best time for you is—in terms of being consistent and in benefitting spiritually. Be honest with yourself. If you need to make some changes so that you do read at the most effective time for you, be willing to make those changes. I promise the effort and any sacrifices will be worth the results. But remember that you might not feel the benefits outweigh the costs the first day . . . or even the thirtieth. Often, our faith must be tried before we receive a confirming witness or see the full benefits (see Ether 12:6).[24]

If you struggle to read the scriptures because you have a hard time understanding them, don't give up! The more you read them, the more you understand. It might help to think of the scriptures as being written in a different language, like French or Russian—one that you've heard spoken before but haven't read. You're likely to have a rough go of it when you first try to understand the writing. But as you keep reading, you'll catch on more and more. As with learning to read another language, it will likely help to take some classes and review resources. In terms of scripture language, the classes include church on Sunday, religious classes during the week, and family discussions. Resources include books and articles that explain the historical and geographic contexts of scriptural books, as well as dictionaries and glossaries that explain the definitions of words that aren't commonly used today.[25] And don't forget about the footnotes in the Book of Mormon, Doctrine and Covenants, Pearl of Great Price, and Latter-day Saint version of the King James Bible. I've gained extensive insight from reading the explanatory notes and turning to the cross-referenced scriptures.

Perhaps the most effective resource we have is prayer. Start your scripture study by praying. Ask Heavenly Father to bless you with the companionship of the Holy Ghost, who is a masterful, patient teacher. He can bring everything to your understanding (see 1 Corinthians 2:9–12; 1 Nephi 10:17, 19; and Moroni 10:5). Don't limit yourself to praying just at the start of your study. Pray throughout, asking for enlightenment when you don't understand a verse. Also ask Heavenly Father how what you're reading relates to your life at this moment. Follow up by asking what actions you need to take based on what you're reading. Finally, remember to thank God for what you've learned from studying and pondering the scriptures with the help of the Holy Ghost. When we express gratitude, we strengthen our relationship with God and Jesus Christ, we're more receptive to what the Holy Ghost wants to teach us, and we're more likely to remember what we've learned.

As we take this approach to reading and pondering the scriptures, we'll come to feast upon them. Let's explore that metaphor of feasting. Imagine the most delectable, satisfying foods you've ever eaten. They're of the highest quality and usually cost more than what you can afford to pay on a regular basis. Though usually reserved for special occasions only, they're all before you on a table, and you can eat as much of any of them as you'd like. Now, if we did that every day, most of us would probably gain unwanted pounds . . . and unwanted health problems. But not so with the scriptures. You can feast on God's word every day without adding an inch to your waistline—or breaking the bank. And you'll feel satisfied, all the while avoiding the stomachache that comes from eating too much scrumptious food.

Why do we need to feast on the scriptures every day? Wouldn't a feast tide us over for at least a few days? Sorry, but no. Since we can't overeat when feasting on the scriptures, we need to refuel every day. I don't know about you, but I get a little testy if I don't eat even every few hours. Going without food for a few days isn't something I want to try, and the same goes for not studying the scriptures for a few days. Reading every day will keep you in the best spiritual shape possible.[26]

Spencer W. Kimball said that when we feast on the scriptures, we acquire greater wisdom to guide our lives and the lives of our families. We also gain a greater ability to let our light shine and to be sources of strength to those in need.[27] Additionally, he noted that by immersing himself in the scriptures, "I find myself loving more intensely those whom I must love with all my heart and mind and strength, and loving them more, I find it easier to abide their counsel."[28] Wow! That result alone would be motivation enough for me to feast on the scriptures.

But there's more. Henry B. Eyring promised that when we consistently feast on the scriptures, they become a part of us.[29] Slowly but surely, I've seen that happen in my life. At various times, a scripture will come to me right when I need it—for my own assistance or to comfort or guide someone else in need. When that happens, I'm not just citing a scripture, I'm drawing on something that I know, something that is part of me.

I feel immense gratitude every day to have joined The Church of Jesus Christ of Latter-day Saints. Through it, I've gained a greater understanding of the blessings that come when I read the scriptures and pray. Of course, being a member of the Church hasn't removed all challenges from my life or from Richard's. The struggles and trials will never end in mortality because through them, we gain the experience needed to become more like Jesus Christ and live with Him again. But when the rain does start to pour and the wind threatens to knock us down, we know where to go for shelter. In addition to the scriptures and prayer, we have the support of our church family— more than fifteen million members strong. They often understand us even better than our blood relatives do and are eager to help at the first mention of a need. It's no wonder that we address each other as "Brother" and "Sister." And of course, we're all children of God, our Heavenly Father.

Notes

1. Think of a century-long game of "Telephone." How could we possibly expect people to retain all parts of the gospel with complete accuracy?
2. And since we're all related to Adam and Eve, we're all related to each other, though in most cases very distantly.
3. The Church of Jesus Christ of Latter-day Saints teaches that children are accountable for their actions (and therefore sins) at the age of eight. An exception is made for those "who are mentally incapable of understanding what is right and what is wrong" (*Gospel Fundamentals*).
4. Here, *Gentiles* essentially means all non-Jews, which includes Christians.
5. The Book of Mormon contains the writings of the Nephites as well as of the Mulekites and the Jaredites. This scripture indicates that other records contain the words of yet other groups.
6. Whether in this life or the next, all of God's children will have the opportunity to learn about and accept His gospel. But whether they do accept, and therefore receive God's greatest blessings, is up to them (see D&C 138, particularly verses 29–35).
7. Some of the sets, at least. I'm still looking forward to the day that we get to read the scriptures God has given to the lost tribes of Israel.
8. In Alma 10:3, we learn that Nephi's father, Lehi, was a descendant of Joseph through his son Manasseh. Lehi's sons married the daughters of Ishmael, who descended from Ephraim, Joseph's other son. Joseph Smith stated that Ishmael's ancestry was explained in the 116 translated pages of the Book of Mormon that Martin Harris lost (Brigham Henry Roberts, *New Witnesses for God: The Book of Mormon*, [Salt Lake City, UT: Deseret News, 1909], 172–73).
9. Howard W. Hunter, "Reading the Scriptures," *Ensign*, November 1979.
10. Robert D. Hales, "Holy Scriptures: The Power of God unto Our Salvation," *Ensign*, November 2006.
11. Richard G. Scott, "The Power of Scripture," *Ensign*, November 2011. I find this last blessing the most intriguing. While I've read research indicating people physically heal faster when they pray, I haven't found any research correlating scripture study and physical healing. For examples of studies that have identified benefits of praying on physical healing, see M. W. Krucoff et al., "Music, Imagery, Touch, and Prayer As Adjuncts to Interventional Cardiac Care: The Monitoring and Actualisation of Noetic Trainings (MANTRA) II Randomised Study, *Lancet* 366 (2005): 211–217; and "Science Proves the Healing Power of Prayer," NewsMax, March 31, 2015, http://www.newsmax.com/Health/Headline/prayer-health-faith-medicine/2015/03/31/id/635623.

12. Hales, "Holy Scriptures: The Power of God unto Our Salvation."
13. See Ezra Taft Benson, "The Book of Mormon: Keystone of Our Religion," *Ensign,* November 1986.
14. For a great discussion on this topic, see L. Tom Perry, "Blessings Resulting from Reading the Book of Mormon," *Ensign,* November 2005.
15. See, for example, 1 Nephi 9:5; 1 Nephi 19:3; and Alma 37:11–12, 14, 18.
16. Joseph Smith's understanding of the book's importance helps explain why he repeatedly risked his life to keep the book safe. For examples, see Andrew H. Hedges, "'Take Heed Continually': Protecting the Gold Plates," *Ensign,* January 2001.
17. See Benson, "The Book of Mormon."
18. See Benson, "The Book of Mormon."
19. Benson, "The Book of Mormon."
20. Henry B. Eyring, "This Day," *Ensign,* May 2007.
21. Joe J. Christensen, "Resolutions" (Brigham Young University devotional, January 9, 1994), 6, speeches.byu.edu.
22. Boyd K. Packer, "Self-Reliance," *Ensign,* August 1975.
23. Packer, "Self-Reliance."
24. Henry B. Eyring explained, "If we choose the right, we will find happiness—in time. If we choose evil, there comes sorrow and regret—in time. Those effects are sure. Yet they are often delayed for a purpose. If the blessings were immediate, choosing the right would not build faith" ("A Priceless Heritage of Hope," *Ensign,* May 2014).
25. Numerous resources are available at www.lds.org. If you want to learn what Latter-day Saint leaders have said about various scripture verses during General Conference, refer to scriptures.byu.edu. If you want to learn more about the context of scriptures in the Doctrine and Covenants and the Pearl of Great Price, you'll love the resources at www.josephsmithpapers.org. You'll also learn more about Joseph Smith as a prophet and as an ordinary man.
26. Likewise, Howard W. Hunter stated, "It is certain that one who studies the scriptures every day accomplishes far more than one who devotes considerable time one day and then lets days go by before continuing" ("Reading the Scriptures").
27. Spencer W. Kimball, "Always a Convert Church: Some Lessons to Learn and Apply This Year," *Ensign,* September 1975.
28. Spencer W. Kimball, *The Teachings of Spencer W. Kimball* (Salt Lake City, UT: Book Craft, 1995), 135.
29. Henry B. Eyring, "A Discussion on Scripture Study," *Ensign,* July 2005.

Chapter 8

SAVIORS ON MOUNT ZION

Junior and Marjorie are absolutely glowing. I'd thought they were glowing during their previous visits with me, but somehow they're even more brilliant now. It's as if they can't contain their joy, so it's bursting out of them in the form of light.

Why are they so happy today? I wonder. Of course, they're always happy, but there's something more today. I didn't think it was possible to be any happier than they'd been before, but Junior and Marjorie are that.

"What's in the suitcase?" It's small—the size of a carry-on. "Are you going on a trip?" Even as I ask, I wonder whether taking a suitcase would be necessary. From what I've seen of heaven, if you need something, you simply think about it and it appears.

"Jane, it's the most wonderful thing ever! We're moving!" Junior exclaimed.

"Moving? What do you mean?" They're already in heaven; certainly they're not moving out (and being kicked out surely wouldn't elicit bliss). So what's going on?

"We're moving to another part of heaven—to a larger mansion filled with more joy and with the presence of God. And it's because you did our temple work!"

I think back to the previous day, when Richard and I reverently entered the Provo Utah Temple to complete beautiful ordinances for Junior and Marjorie. I was beginning to understand why they were

⌒ 85 ⌒

elated. Richard and I had felt the same way just a few weeks earlier, when we'd completed the temple ordinances for ourselves. Our experience in the temple was indescribable—such joy, peace, and intense feelings of God's love as I had only felt long before during my first experience in heaven.

But I still wonder, *What's the deal with the suitcase?* Marjorie sees me eying it. "We packed up all our belongings," she says.

"So where's everything else?"

"Oh, it all fit in the one suitcase."

Now I'm even more confused. I've heard of packing lightly, but Junior and Marjorie have taken it to a new level.

Marjorie laughs as she takes the suitcase from Junior and sets it in front of me. "Jane, let me show you what's inside. Then you'll understand."

She unzips the suitcase, and as can only happen in heaven, a mansion emerges. It's like Mary Poppins pulling something out of her traveling bag, but on a humongous scale.

I finally stop staring at the mansion, which is considerably larger and more impressive than where Junior and Marjorie were living before. I turn to them and see tears streaming down their cheeks. "Thank you, Jane," Junior tells me.

Marjorie nods her head and sniffs. "Yes, thank you. It's because of you and Richard—because you completed ordinances for us in the temple. We can't thank you enough."

With how my life has changed because of them, I can't thank them enough either. Not only am I immeasurably happier with my life, but I also have a magnificent eternal life to look forward to in heaven. A life that I'll spend with my family—never to be parted— because of making and keeping temple ordinances.

One of the most glorious concepts the missionaries taught Richard and me is that families can be together forever. Of course, I already knew that—Richard's father shared that truth during his first visit with me. But it was thrilling to hear the missionaries explain exactly how families can live together for eternity. The key, I learned, is the sealing power that only exists in God's holy temples. Families can be sealed together for eternity after each family member has been baptized and then completed sacred preparatory ordinances in a temple. Richard and I had already accomplished the first step: being baptized. Our next step was to prepare to enter the temple.

LDS temples are beautiful, sacred places because of what happens in them. There's a lot of speculation about exactly what does go on in temples because those who enter are asked not to share specifics. For this reason, some people have assumed that temple activities must be weird or inappropriate. But that's not the case. The reason for not discussing details outside of the temple is because they are so special—so sacred—that they need to be treated with utmost reverence. It's similar to the reason why we've been commanded not to use God's name in vain. He is sacred, and using His name for common (and unfortunately often vulgar) purposes desecrates His name and shows a lack of respect and love. To keep what happens in the temple sacred, we're instructed to discuss the temple with great reverence. Much of what goes on is holy and should only be discussed in a holy place—namely, the temple.

That's the same reason why people must meet certain requirements before attending the temple. When I was being taught about the temple, I learned that before I could enter and complete ordinances for myself, I would need to be a member of The Church of Jesus Christ of Latter-day Saints for at least one year. The purpose of the rule isn't to be exclusionary but rather to help ensure I was adequately prepared in the gospel to understand and live the principles taught in the temple. I would also need to complete a series of confidential interviews with local Church leaders to determine whether I was prepared and personally worthy to enter the temple. I would need to answer questions such as whether I had a testimony of Jesus Christ, supported Church leaders, paid tithing, observed the law of chastity, and kept other commandments. If my answers indicated I met the requirements, I would receive a temple recommend, giving me access to the temple.[1]

For those who are new to the concept of LDS temples and temple recommends, it may be helpful to consider an object lesson Gordon B. Hinckley, fifteenth President and Prophet of the Church, shared. He began, "I hold before you two credit cards"—one being a temple recommend and the other a card issued by a bank. Of the bank credit card he said, "In accepting it from my bank, I enter into a contract and become bound by obligations and agreements. In accepting the card, I agree to meet the conditions under which it was issued. . . . It is not really mine. The bank retains ownership. If I fail in my required performance, then the bank may shut off the credit and repossess the card." Similarly, a temple recommend "represents a credit card with the Lord, making available to me many of His greatest gifts. . . . To secure a temple recommend, the receiver must also have demonstrated his eligibility, and that eligibility is based on personal worthiness. . . . It is subject to forfeiture if the holder does anything which would disqualify him for its privileges."[2]

With a temple recommend, I would be able to enter the temple to participate in baptisms for deceased family members as well as to complete additional ordinances, first for myself and then for the deceased.[3] The ordinances include washings, anointings, clothing in garments of the priesthood, an endowment of power, and a sealing that binds together family members on earth and in heaven. Did you know that the scriptures talk about some of these ordinances? Let's take a look.

In 1 Corinthians 15:29, Paul poses the following question: "Else what shall they do which are baptized for the dead, if the dead rise not at all? why are they then baptized for the dead?" While I've heard this verse interpreted various ways by people of other religions, it's clear to me that the early Christian church—as in shortly after Christ died and before the doctrines were polluted and diluted—believed in and engaged in baptisms for the dead.[4]

In Exodus 40:12–15, God directed Moses to "bring Aaron and his sons unto the door of the tabernacle of the congregation [i.e., a portable temple], and wash them with water. And thou shalt put upon Aaron the holy garments, and anoint him, and sanctify him; that he may minister unto me in the priest's office. And thou shalt bring his sons, and clothe them with coats: And thou shalt anoint them . . . for their anointing shall surely be an everlasting priesthood throughout their generations." Similarly, in LDS temples today, adults who enter the temple to receive their endowment are first washed, anointed, sanctified, and clothed in holy garments. Elsewhere in the Bible are references to washings and anointings, though not in a temple context. Yet these references provide insight into the purpose of the washing and anointing ordinances in the temple. For example, washing often symbolizes cleansing a person from sin and the pollutions of the world, while anointing symbolizes sanctification, purification, consecration, and healing.[5]

True, these references are brief and general. But that's for good reason. Because of the temple's sacred nature, the details of these ordinances shouldn't be discussed outside of the temple. However, leaders of the Church have felt it appropriate to provide some more information than what we have in the scriptures, and I'm going to share a sampling with you. Hopefully, what I discuss here will give you a good idea of why Latter-day Saints love the temple. Truly, there's nowhere on Earth that I'd rather be, especially if family members and dear friends are with me.

After an individual completes what are called initiatory ordinances (the washing, anointing, and clothing mentioned in Exodus 40), then he or she is ready to participate in the endowment ordinance. "To endow is to enrich, to give to another something long lasting and of much worth." The temple endowment enriches in multiple ways. For example, the person participating in this ordinance receives power from God and an education in God's plan and purposes, including the essential role of Jesus Christ in atoning for our sins.[6] The Church has taught, "The temple endowment teaches us many things that we must know and do in order to return to our Father in Heaven. During the endowment we also promise the Lord to obey the laws of sacrifice and chastity and to be willing to give everything we have to help in His work."[7] Apostle James E. Talmage added that "with the taking of each covenant and the assuming of each obligation a promised blessing is pronounced, contingent upon the faithful observance of the conditions."[8]

The crowning ordinance in the temple is the sealing, which involves connecting (or sealing) husband, wife, and children for eternity. The word *sealing* is quite appropriate in my opinion. It means to tightly and perfectly close something, to make secure or guarantee,[9] suggesting the connection can't be broken. And it won't be, unless we choose to break the seal by disobeying God's commandments and choosing not to repent. Doctrine and Covenants 128:9 talks about the power to seal: "It may seem to some to be a very bold doctrine that we talk of—a power which records or binds on earth and binds in heaven. Nevertheless, in all ages of the world, whenever the Lord has given a dispensation of the priesthood to any man by actual revelation, or any set of men, this power has always been given." We have record of that in Matthew 16:13–19, when Jesus Christ told Peter, "And I will give unto thee the keys of the kingdom of heaven: and whatsoever thou shalt bind on earth shall be bound in heaven: and whatsoever thou shalt loose on earth shall be loosed in heaven" (see also Helaman 10:7). The priesthood power Jesus gave Peter to bind on earth and in heaven is the same priesthood power Joseph Smith received, and that authority has been passed down to succeeding prophets, apostles, and those select few who are called to officiate as temple sealers.[10]

According to Paul Hyer, "Sealings endow life with greater purpose and give marriage a sense of divine partnership with spiritual safeguards. Bringing children into the world becomes a divinely inspired stewardship. Sealings can sustain a family in life and console them in death" because of the knowledge that family members will be together in heaven.[11]

Being with my family for eternity is reason enough to be sealed in the temple and then to always honor my temple covenants so that the sealing remains in force. But there's more. God is amazingly generous and eager to offer His children more than we deserve or can even imagine. This fact is perhaps most apparent in the gifts He promises to give us if we're sealed in the temple and stay true to our covenants: "If a man marry a wife by my word . . . and by the new and everlasting covenant [the temple sealing] . . . [they] shall inherit thrones, kingdoms, principalities, and powers, dominions, all heights and depths . . . and they shall pass by the angels, and the gods, which are set there, to their exaltation and glory in all things, as hath been sealed upon their heads, which glory shall be a fullness" (D&C 132:19). How beautiful those blessings are! Truly, there is nothing greater—it's the promise that we and our family members can become joint-heirs with Christ. And the temple ordinances are the only way we can obtain God's greatest gifts.

Family is at the center of the promises available through making temple covenants. And those promises aren't limited to blessings in heaven. Many of the blessings are available now. Elder Richard H. Winkel said that "when you come to the temple you will love your family with a deeper love than you have ever felt before."[12] I know that to be true—I've seen it time and again since I first entered the temple. Apostle Richard G. Scott explained that attending the temple can also strengthen relationships with family members who have already died.[13] I believe Elder Scott speaks from experience. In an address he once gave, he explained that his beloved wife, Jeanene, had died fourteen years prior. In the same address, he noted that he'd started attending the temple weekly fourteen years before.[14] I don't think it's a coincidence that he began attending the temple more frequently around the time he lost his wife. I believe one of the reasons he increased his temple attendance was because of the beautiful ways the temple reminds us "that covenants made in the temple are eternal," meaning families can be together forever.[15]

I've been reminded of that truth time and again as I've attended the temple to complete ordinances for deceased family members. We can only be together if all temple ordinances have been completed, so it's essential that we do this work on behalf of ancestors who didn't have the chance to enter the temple during their lives. God knew that millions—even billions—of His children wouldn't have the opportunity to accept His gospel while living. So many people have lived at times when the complete gospel, including each temple ordinance, wasn't on the earth. Even when these ordinances have been available, numerous people have never heard about Christianity, let alone The Church of Jesus Christ of Latter-day Saints. Our Heavenly Father is loving and just—He won't bar anyone from inheriting all He has just because they didn't have the opportunity to learn about and accept His gospel while in mortality. So He gives everyone a chance after they die. Missionary work is a huge part of life in heaven. People are either teaching the gospel or learning about it. Of course, those who accept the gospel in heaven aren't able to return to mortality in order to complete temple ordinances. That's where we come in. We can serve as proxy for them in the temple, completing each ordinance essential to obtaining God's highest blessings—including an eternal family. This work is a fulfillment of Malachi's prophecy that Elijah would "turn the heart of the fathers to the children, and the heart of the children to their fathers" (Malachi 4:6). It's also what Paul was talking about when he said that "they [our ancestors] without us should not be made perfect" (Hebrews 11:40).[16] God's plan makes my heart thrill; He is so wise and kind.[17]

To some people, the idea of completing others' temple ordinances by proxy may seem strange. Or pointless. Does it really do any good? Joseph Fielding Smith addressed this very issue:

> I have heard it said many times by those who oppose this work that it is impossible for one person to stand vicariously for another. Those who express themselves in this way overlook the fact that the entire work of salvation is a vicarious work, Jesus Christ standing as the propitiator, redeeming us from death, for which we were not responsible, and also redeeming us from the responsibility of our own sins, on condition of our repentance and acceptance of the gospel. He has done this on a grand infinite scale and by the same principle he has delegated authority to the members of his Church to act for the dead who are helpless to perform the saving ordinances for themselves.[18]

Christ gave Peter, James, and John authority to act in His name, and He likewise gives us authority to act on behalf of those who didn't have the opportunity to be baptized and receive essential temple ordinances during mortality. This vicarious work is the reason Jesus could be just in telling Nicodemus, "Except a man be born of water and of the Spirit, he cannot enter into the kingdom of God" (John 3:5).

Since I started doing my ancestors' temple ordinances—and completing the prerequisite genealogy work—I've been able to feel the influence of my deceased family members strongly in my life. I feel their presence, and they help me find more ancestors, allowing me to complete even more relatives' temple ordinances. Sometimes it seems like I can almost hear their voices, whispering names to me or telling me where to look for more genealogical information. On many occasions I've heard the plea, "Do my work! Please, do my work!" When I've finished the genealogical work for ancestors and am ready to serve as proxy in the temple, I can feel their excitement, hope, and love. They know that soon they'll be packing up all their possessions in a suitcase and moving to a mansion that exceeds their wildest expectations. Those feelings are even stronger after I enter the temple and participate in the ordinances. I know they're in the temple with me, listening to the beautiful covenants I'm making with God on their behalf. I feel them hugging me, and their happiness and gratitude overwhelm me. I feel as if I'm going to burst with joy. Sometimes I'll see glimpses of angels and light. It's like a blissful burst of warm sunshine. And I know that the temple is filled with many more angels than I can see. So many family members—not just mine, but those of everyone in the temple—are ecstatic that their time has finally come, that they finally have the opportunity to fulfill all of the requirements to receive exaltation with God and Jesus Christ.

With such euphoric experiences, it's no wonder that when I leave the temple, people often tell me I'm glowing. But I'm not unique in that. Anyone who enters the temple with a pure heart and a desire to do temple work for the deceased can't help but be filled with light while in the temple. God's house is filled with light, just as He is, and we receive a portion of that light when we visit. I personally believe that the light we carry from the temple is one of the reasons many people of other faiths have noted that Latter-day Saints have a light about them.[19]

Many times, after I've witnessed my ancestors celebrate in the temple, they've also visited me that night in my dreams. With tears flowing down their cheeks, they've thanked me, just as Junior and Marjorie did, for being a savior on Mount Zion for them.[20] Through completing the sealing ordinance for them, I've linked them to their ancestors and descendants. That means we'll all be together in heaven, in one long, glorious family chain, never to be broken.

According to Church doctrine, there are three degrees or levels of glory in heaven: telestial, terrestrial, and celestial (see D&C 76; 1 Corinthians 15:40–42). Even the lowest kingdom is beyond all mortal expectation, but the celestial kingdom is where we should all aspire to go because it's the kingdom filled with the glory and presence of Heavenly Father and Jesus Christ (see D&C 76:62, 89).[21] Because "no unclean thing can enter into [this] kingdom" (3 Nephi 37:19), qualifying for celestial glory requires repenting, receiving a testimony of Jesus Christ and His true gospel, being baptized, and accepting all of the ordinances in the temple. That's why Junior and Marjorie appeared to me one night with their suitcase and tears of joy streaming down their cheeks. They were moving to a higher level of heaven because Richard and I had completed their temple work and they had accepted it. They were clean and were ready to receive their celestial glory.

According to Church doctrine, until Christ's final judgment, deceased individuals live in the postmortal spirit world. This postmortal world is a form of heaven but not the celestial, terrestrial, and telestial kingdoms. Based on my dreams, I believe the postmortal spirit world somewhat mirrors the kingdoms of glory. When Junior and Marjorie accepted the baptisms Richard and I completed for them, they moved to a bigger, nicer home in the postmortal world. When we completed their other temple work, they packed their suitcase once again and moved into an even nicer home—a mansion. This mansion provides a glimpse of what they'll receive when they enter the celestial kingdom.

Because people in heaven are at different stages of learning about and accepting the gospel and ordinances, they live in different areas of heaven. That includes family members; they're not prevented from seeing each other, but it takes time and effort. Before Richard and I were baptized for Junior and Marjorie, I saw them travel in covered wagons to visit other family members. After all of their ordinances were completed, they could visit family members with a simple thought. They'd automatically appear at the home of whatever family members they wanted to see. Also, family members who had similarly received their temple covenants lived in the same area of heaven, often next door to each other. The number of family members who live close by in heaven continues to increase as Richard and I complete the temple work for more of them. Around the beginning of each year, I have a dream where the extended family takes a big trip, and it's thrilling to see how the size of the group is bigger each time—all because their temple ordinances have been completed.

It does take some family members longer than others to be ready to accept the gospel and the sacred ordinances that have been completed for them. I learned that in a dream involving Paul.

"Paul's here!" Marjorie tells me as I walk into the entryway of the mansion she shares with Junior.

Her excitement is infectious, and it runs through me. This is great news! But . . . who *is* Paul? Have I met him? Has Marjorie mentioned him before? She's so excited, I'm sure he's family, but I still have no clue who he is.

"Oh, sorry, Jane," Marjorie says. "I'm just so happy that I forgot we've never talked to you about him before." She pauses, and I can tell she's trying to decide where to start.

"Well . . ." she trails off.

My curiosity increases as I wait for her to explain, wondering why she seems unsure of what to say.

"Well," she begins again. "I almost don't want to even mention it since it doesn't matter anymore. He's repented and is here with us now. That's what's important."

Now she's *really* got my attention. "What—" I stop myself. I want to know what she's talking about, but I don't want to push if she doesn't feel comfortable telling me. I see a movement behind her, and my eyes shift to the three men walking toward me. One of them is Junior, but I haven't met the other two before.

"Hi, Jane," Junior greets me. After wrapping me in a hug, he gestures to the taller of the two men at his side. "This is my oldest brother, Harold." Harold gives me a glowing smile, and then Junior turns to the other man. "And this is his son, Paul."

"It's wonderful to meet you both," I say. And I mean it. I already love them so much, even though I've just met them. Heaven has a way of doing that, especially when it comes to family.

"You can get acquainted while we eat lunch," Marjorie says as she ushers us into the dining room. A tantalizing spread of food has been laid out, and we don't waste time filling our plates. As we dig in, Harold entertains me with stories from Richard's childhood.

I'm so riveted by the stories, I lose track of time. But then I notice Junior looking at his watch. I know what that means. It's time for me to wake up back in the mortal world.

I slowly opened my eyes and stifled a yawn. Richard was standing by the bed. "I met your uncle Harold," I said as I sat up. "He's simply captivating. He told me all kinds of stories about you. Like teaching you and your sister how to play Marco Polo in your swimming pool."

"Yeah, I'd forgotten about that," Richard said with a chuckle. He grinned and his eyes lost focus, and I could tell he was thinking of fond memories that involved his uncle.

Though he was obviously enjoying the memories, I decided to interrupt his thoughts. I was impatient to tell him about the rest of my dream—and maybe get some answers.

"I also met Paul. He just got there."

Well, I certainly succeeded in capturing Richard's attention. He looked me in the eyes, but I couldn't quite interpret the look on his face. Sadness? Pain? Maybe even some fear and anger?

I reluctantly continued. "Everyone was so happy for him to be there. Apparently, Harold's been waiting for quite a while. I'm not sure where Paul was before or why he didn't arrive sooner. From the bits and pieces I heard, I think it has to do with the way he and Harold died."

I paused then because Richard had started pacing the room.

"Richard, are you okay?"

"Yes," he said, but I could tell he wasn't. I remained quiet, waiting for him to say something.

Finally, he broke the silence. "Jane, it doesn't make sense. Harold and Paul died on the same night. Their house burned down . . . and we think it was Paul's fault, that he'd been smoking in bed.

How terrible. Now I understood why Marjorie was reluctant to tell me what had happened. Though Paul surely didn't mean to catch the house on fire and take his father's and his own life, that's what his negligence had led to.

As time went on and I learned more about Paul and about the Church's teachings on the postmortal spirit world, I came to understand that Paul needed time to repent of his mistakes and prepare to accept Christ's gospel. While it took him longer than it took some of his family members, he was eventually ready. And that's when he was able to join them. Paul's story is one of mercy, patience, and hope. Truly, God prepares a way for people to be forgiven of their sins and to be reunited with family members.

As I've mentioned previously, temple work and genealogical work are connected. Without completing genealogical work, we won't know who our ancestors are and therefore won't be able to complete their temple ordinances. Family history has increased my awareness of being a member of a family. Not just a member of my immediate family but of a family larger than I can really comprehend—after all, every genealogical line eventually traces back to Adam and Eve. We're all related, and I want all of us to be sealed together. That's why I'm compelled to do family history work for my relatives—and then to make sure my ancestors' temple ordinances are completed.

Some people, maybe even you, believe that family history work is the less-exciting part. When you think of researching your family line, you might envision looking through roll after roll of microfilm, hour after hour, just to come up empty. Well, I'll agree that the process can be challenging, but it's also changed so much from twenty years ago—even ten years ago! You don't need to travel to a genealogical library anymore. All you need is a computer and an internet connection, and you have hundreds of tools and millions of names at your fingertips. No more need to sit in front of a microfilm reader. Enter a name into a search bar, and you'll be impressed by all the relevant information you'll have in ten seconds.

True, once the search results appear, you still have to look through them. The names won't actually find themselves and start flashing in red to get your attention (though I'm still holding out hope that technology will get that good). I see family history work as an opportunity to play detective. And who hasn't wanted to do that at least once? I've actually found the work addictive—in a good way. The more I do it, the more I want to do it.

Even if you've never tried before, don't let that stop you. The LDS Church's FamilySearch program (familysearch.org) is continually being improved and making genealogical work simpler—easy enough that children can teach you how to start. You can also review numerous step-by-step tutorials.[22] Trust me, no one would ever call me a computer expert, but I've been able to master FamilySearch. You can too.

New records are being added all the time, so if you can't find information on a family member today, check back next week. I've done that more than once, and I've been thrilled to find the last puzzle piece—a missing name or date—that I needed before I could complete someone's temple ordinances. And don't forget to pray for help. As with any other righteous desire, God will answer your prayers. Sometimes the help you ask for will come through your ancestors. More than once, ancestors have whispered to me where I needed to look to find their information. As Richard G. Scott explained, "This work is a spiritual work, a monumental effort of cooperation on both sides of the veil, where help is given in both directions. Anywhere you are in the world, with prayer, faith, determination, diligence, and some sacrifice, you can make a powerful contribution. Begin now. I promise you that the Lord will help you find a way. And it will make you feel wonderful."[23]

Deceased family members on my side and on Richard's side have begged me to do family history work in preparation for serving as proxy for them in temple ordinances. I know your ancestors are making the same plea. I realize that not everyone is able to hear the plea as clearly as I do. If you need more motivation, remember what God said through Malachi: "Behold, I will send you Elijah the prophet before the coming of the great and dreadful day of the Lord: And he shall turn the heart of the fathers to the children, and the heart of the children to their fathers, lest I come and smite the earth with a curse" (Malachi 4:5–6). Yes, it's that important. So if you aren't involved in genealogy already, please join me in God's work.

When Richard and I first learned that we could not only change our lives but also the lives of our ancestors through temple work, we were humbled—we could help our deceased family members just as they had been helping us by leading us on a journey to The Church of Jesus Christ of Latter-day Saints. But Richard was also a little worried that he might offend deceased family members by completing their temple ordinances. As recent converts, we still had a lot of questions. Soon after, we attended a special Church meeting where Apostle David A. Bednar spoke. It was as if he were speaking directly to us, addressing all of our uncertainties. Elder Bednar explained that our ancestors aren't forced to accept the ordinances we complete for them—God never takes away anyone's agency. By completing their ordinances, we're giving them an opportunity they wouldn't have otherwise. An opportunity to accept Jesus Christ's gospel and the ordinances required to live with Him in heaven.

While no one is forced to accept the work we do in the temple, I have no doubt that most embrace the ordinances. They are anxiously waiting for their work to be completed. Many of them have been ready for a long time. They received their gospel instruction in heaven from angels who've already received temple ordinances. We don't need to worry about that part—our responsibility is to provide them with the opportunity to accept the gospel by completing their temple ordinances.

Beyond the incomparable blessings the temple provides in terms of family, the temple is also a place of refuge when we feel burdened with trials, when our hearts are hurting, and when we have important decisions to make. The temple is the House of the Lord, meaning we can go there to feel His peace, His love, and His guidance. Going to the temple helps me keep the right perspective. When I think my challenges are more than I can bear, I attend the temple and am reminded that Christ has experienced my tribulations and will support me through them. When I'm stressed about all I need to accomplish or the fires that I need to put out, I attend the temple and am reminded that most of those things don't matter. They'll get done, and a month or a year from now, the fires will even seem trivial. When I'm impatient to receive promised blessings, I attend the temple and am reminded that the blessings will come—according to Heavenly Father's timing. That timing may not be until heaven, but from the eternal perspective I gain in the temple, waiting until then is manageable; this mortal life is so short in comparison. When it feels that all the world is in commotion, I attend the temple and feel the peace that only God and Jesus Christ can provide. At these times, I never want to leave His holy house. It is the closest that we can get to heaven while still in this life of trials, uncertainty, upheaval, and imperfection.

Through attending the temple, our love of Jesus Christ and Heavenly Father will increase. We'll also feel greater love for those around us—even those we may consider our enemies. Attending the temple, particularly to complete ordinances for our ancestors, will also protect us from the evil that abounds in this world.[24]

Now, a word of caution: because the temple is God's holy house, the only place we can make certain essential covenants with Him, and a place of refuge, Satan obviously doesn't want us to enter this most sacred of places. He will go to great lengths to stop us from entering the temple—for the first time and ever afterward. I know that from personal experience and from talking with many other people. As I was preparing to enter the temple to complete the initiatory ordinances and the endowment for myself, I was more excited than I can put into words. I knew that there wasn't anything more important that I could do in my life. And for that very reason, Satan started putting roadblocks in my way, just as he does with everyone.

Though Satan is waging a full-out war, we often don't notice his strategies for what they are. They're often very sneaky. It might be that we have car troubles or something else comes up in the hours before we've scheduled to visit the temple. Maybe we start to feel very tired and are tempted to lie down instead of entering God's house. Whatever Satan's tactic might be at a particular time, recognize it for what it is, and determine that you're not going to let him win! We always have the power to conquer the devil—unless we willingly give it away, consciously or unconsciously submitting to him.[25] Once you realize what's happening, ask Heavenly Father for help. He wants you to enter the temple as often as possible, meaning He'll help you to make it . . . if you ask.

One morning, I was looking forward to go to the temple after work that day. Something came up before I even made it to the office. I have no recollection of what the problem was, but I do remember that I felt stressed, thinking my plans to attend the temple were foiled. But then I realized I had other options. I could choose not to let Satan prevent me from doing what I wanted and needed to do. So I started to pray. I told Heavenly Father that I really wanted to go to the temple that day but I didn't see how it was possible. I asked Him to help me know how I could resolve the issues I was facing so that I wouldn't have to forego my trip to His holy house. And He answered. Soon, inspiration started coming to me. I understood what I needed to do so that I could take care of the unplanned roadblock *and* make it to the temple that night.

In sharing that story, I think it's important to point out a few things. I recognize that sometimes things will come up that prevent us from following through on our intent to visit the temple, and even if we pray for help, we may still have to delay our plans. In my case,

God knew there was a relatively simple way for me to address the little emergency that came up, enabling me to go to the temple that day. In other situations, Heavenly Father might answer our prayers by telling us to focus on the problem in front of us today so that we can make it to the temple tomorrow . . . or next week . . . or whatever His timing is. He wants us to attend the temple as often as possible, but He understands our circumstances—even better than we do.

I certainly don't think I would have been sinning if I hadn't gone to the temple that day. But I wouldn't have been living up to my full potential, and my faith wouldn't have been strengthened if I hadn't asked Heavenly Father for help. I wouldn't necessarily have been moving backward spiritually, but I wouldn't have been moving forward, and we always need to be moving forward if we want to overcome Satan's temptations and eventually inherit all that God has for those who are faithful to Him.[26] I also believe that when we let Satan score once, it's more likely that we'll let him score another point, and then another and another. It seems that every day of my life is filled with surprises that could derail me from focusing on what God wants me to do: attending the temple, reading my scriptures, praying, and serving others, to name a few.

If you're like me, there's no end of reasons that could prevent you from doing these things. Maybe your boss threw a work project at you that has to be finished *today*, meaning you'll be working late. Or maybe you get a flat tire. Or perhaps your fridge stops working and you have to wait for a technician to come check it out. Those are all legitimate issues to address, and we could use them to rationalize not having time to read the scriptures, attend the temple, and do other things that Christ has asked us to do. And, of course, rationalizing is one of Satan's favorite tactics. He knows that if we start rationalizing, then our habits of doing the right things may turn into habits of *not* doing those things.

Now, I'm not saying that all is lost if you miss one trip to the temple or one day of scripture reading.[27] But Satan takes whatever opportunities he can to change your good habits and turn you away from God. So leave him as few opportunities as possible. Make the commitment to yourself, to God, and to others[28] that you won't let the unexpected—or the expected—keep you from doing what God has asked you to do, including going to the temple.

One final lesson I learned is that I need to act. I truly wanted to attend the temple that day, so I took action. That action involved asking God for help and then following the guidance He gave me. If I hadn't taken those two actions, I wouldn't have made it to the temple. Heavenly Father wanted me to go, and He knew I had the same desire, but He wasn't going to prevent problems from getting in my way. If He did that, we'd never experience any challenges and the consequent opportunities to grow and become stronger and more faithful. But when we ask for help, He will deliver us.[29] As I said before, His deliverance may not come the very day we ask for it, but it will come—at the time He knows is just right.[30]

I know I was blessed with more spiritual strength that day because I acted. I also gained a stronger testimony that God wants us to regularly spend time in the temple and that He'll help us make that happen. The experience also reinforced my faith that Heavenly Father listens to our prayers and is eager to answer them.

Notes

1. I love how God has established the requirements for entering the temple. He doesn't expect us to be perfect to enter His house; rather, we enter the temple to be perfected. But to enter, we do need to be trying to be the best we can, which we demonstrate by keeping His commandments and repenting when we lapse. (See "Being Worthy to Enter the Temple," *Ensign,* August 2010.)
2. Gordon B. Hinckley, "Keeping the Temple Holy," *Ensign,* May 1990.
3. Prior to being a member of the Church for a year, I could obtain a "limited-use" temple recommend to perform baptisms for the dead. Church members can obtain this kind of recommend as long as they are at least twelve years old and demonstrate their worthiness in the two interviews with leaders.
4. Although 1 Corinthians 15:29 is the only biblical reference to baptisms for the dead, other early Christian literature confirms that followers of

Christ performed this important work (David L. Paulsen and Brock M. Mason, "Baptism for the Dead in Early Christianity," *Journal of the Book of Mormon and Other Restoration Scripture* 19, no. 2 [2010]: 22–49). For a discussion of similarities between ancient temples and LDS temples and what goes on in them, see Stephen D. Ricks, "Temples: Temples through the Ages," in *Encyclopedia of Mormonism*, ed. Daniel H. Ludlow, http://eom.byu.edu/index.php/Temples#Temples:_Temples_Through_the_Ages.

5. For scriptures on washing, see Psalm 51:7; Isaiah 1:16; 4:4; John 13:5–10; and 1 Corinthians 6:11. For scriptures on anointing, see Exodus 28:41; Leviticus 8:10–12; and James 5:14. See also Doctrine and Covenants 88:138–139 and Donald W. Parry, "Washings and Anointings," in *Encyclopedia of Mormonism*, ed. Daniel H. Ludlow, http://eom.byu.edu/index.php/Washings_and_Anointings.

6. Boyd K. Packer, "Come to the Temple," *Ensign,* October 2007.

7. The Church of Jesus Christ of Latter-day Saints, *Duties and Blessings of the Priesthood: Basic Manual for Priesthood Holders, Part B.* (Salt Lake City, UT: The Church of Jesus Christ of Latter-day Saints, 2000), 33.

8. James E. Talmage, *The House of the Lord: A Study of Holy Sanctuaries, Ancient and Modern* (Salt Lake City, UT: Deseret News, 1912), 100.

9. *Merriam-Webster Online,* s.v. "Seal."

10. When a couple is sealed in the temple, any children they have afterward are born in "the covenant," meaning they are automatically part of the sealing that binds the family together. If a couple has had children before being sealed, then the children can be sealed to their parents at the time that their parents are sealed in the temple.

11. Paul V. Hyer, "Sealing: Temple Sealings," in *Encyclopedia of Mormonism*, ed. Daniel H. Ludlow, http://eom.byu.edu/index.php/Sealing#Sealing:_Temple_Sealings.

12. Richard H. Winkel, "The Temple Is about Families," *Ensign,* November 2006.

13. Richard G. Scott, "How to Obtain Revelation and Inspiration for Your Personal Life," *Ensign,* May 2012.

14. Richard G. Scott, "Temple Worship: The Source of Strength and Power in Times of Need," *Ensign,* May 2009.

15. Scott, "How to Obtain Revelation and Inspiration for Your Personal Life."

16. For the context, see verses 35–39. Joseph Smith added that "neither can we without them be made perfect" (D&C 128:15).

17. To learn more about temple work for the dead and the joy this message brings, see Doctrine and Covenants 128.

18. Joseph Fielding Smith, *The Restoration of All Things* (Salt Lake City, UT: Deseret News Press, 1945), 174–175.

19. The phenomenon even has a name: Mormon Glow. For examples, see James E. Faust, "The Light in Their Eyes," *Ensign,* November 2005, and "What's in a Face?" *Psychology Today,* November 5, 2012, https://www.psychologytoday.com/articles/201211/whats-in-face.

20. See The Church of Jesus Christ of Latter-day Saints, *Teachings of Presidents of the Church: Joseph Smith* (Salt Lake City, UT: The Church of Jesus Christ of Latter-day Saints, 2011), 472–473; and Obadiah 1:21.

21. Those in the terrestrial kingdom will have the opportunity to dwell in Christ's presence, but not God's. Those in the telestial kingdom will enjoy the Holy Ghost's presence, but not that of Heavenly Father and Jesus Christ. Individuals in both kingdoms will receive the ministrations of those in higher kingdoms (see D&C 76:77, 86–88).

22. Susan C. Milliner, "FamilySearch Online Training Is a Click Away," March 11, 2014, https://beta.familysearch.org/blog/en/familysearch-online-training-click.

23. Richard G. Scott, "The Joy of Redeeming the Dead," *Ensign,* November 2012.

24. See *Come unto Christ through Temple Ordinances and Covenants* (pamphlet, 1987).

25. See *Teachings of Presidents of the Church: Joseph Smith* (2011), 211, 214.

26. According to Elder Kim B. Clark, "Whatever level of spirituality or faith or obedience we now have, it will not be sufficient for the work that lies ahead. We need greater spiritual light and power. We need eyes to see more clearly the Savior working in our lives and ears to hear His voice more deeply in our hearts" ("Eyes to See and Ears to Hear," *Ensign,* November 2015). That means we always need to be moving forward. Remaining stationery isn't enough. See also Neil L. Andersen, "A Compensatory Spiritual Power for the Righteous" (Brigham Young University devotional, August 18, 2015), speeches.byu.edu.

27. In fact, all is never lost. See, for example, Elaine S. Dalton, "Be Not Moved," *Ensign,* May 2013, and Tad R. Callister, in "Christ's Atonement Triumphed over Four Obstacles," by Valerie Johnson, *Church News,* March 30, 2015, https://www.lds.org/church/news/christs-atonement-triumphed-over-four-obstacles.

28. A lot of research shows that when we share our goals with other people, we feel more accountable and are therefore more likely to keep our

commitments and achieve our goals. See, for example, Lisa Evans, "Why Sharing Your Progress Makes You More Likely to Accomplish Your Goals," Fast Company, June 19, 2015, http://www.fastcompany .com/3047432/work-smart/why-sharing-your-progress-makes-you -more-likely-to-accomplish-your-goals. When you share your temple goals with others, why not invite them to make temple goals of their own? If you plan to go together, then you can help each other overcome any roadblocks that appear.

29. Elder Randall K. Bennett declared that when we act in faith, "The Lord more than matches our willingness to act in faith. Our willingness to take a step is not just met; it is exceeded by the Lord's promised blessings" ("Your Next Step," *Ensign,* November 2015).

30. In the last few months as I've studied the Book of Mormon, I've noticed many examples of how God has delivered His children when they were humble, were repentant, and asked Him for help. While sometimes the deliverance was immediate, many times there was a waiting period. Not because He enjoyed watching them suffer for a while or because He felt a sense of satisfaction, as we mortals sometimes do, thinking, *Hey, you got yourself into a pickle, so it serves you right that you have to suffer for a time.* He delivers us the very second after we've learned what we needed to or otherwise experienced what He knew was for our best eternal good. Some of my favorite verses on being delivered, including the waiting process, are in Mosiah chapter 24, particularly verses 12–16. To expand your study, start with Mosiah chapter 21 and read to the end of that book. Then, read the entire Book of Mormon with a focus on noticing God's deliverance. I think you'll be surprised just how often the topic comes up.

Chapter 9

A Mighty Change of Heart

My mom is standing in front of my childhood home in Oskaloosa, Iowa. Wow, she looks so young, maybe in her early thirties. My memories of that long ago are vague, but I do remember that our house was down the street from a small store, and sometimes parents would park on our street and run into the market for a few items, leaving their children in the car. (In the 1950s, stranger danger wasn't as much of an issue as it is today.) As if confirming my recollection, an approaching car slows down and pulls to the side of the road. A woman hops out, looks both ways, and then rushes across the street to the store. I can see three young children in the back seat. What I see next grips my heart with fear. The street has a steady decline, and the car is starting to roll down. Not only are the children in danger, but so is anyone in the car's path. I feel helpless, knowing that in this dream of a past situation, I can't do anything to help.

That's when I hear my mom's scream. I see her racing for the car and yelling for my dad to help. She reaches the car and yanks on the door handle. With the car moving, she stumbles as she tries to climb in and put her foot on the brake. My dad's voice reaches my ears. He's almost to the car and is shouting directions to my mom.

It's going to be okay, I tell myself. *It's going to be okay.*

But I realize I'm wrong as I see the car flip, trapping my mom underneath.

"No! Mom!" I scream. I clasp my hands tightly in front of my mouth, and I continue watching, too stunned to cry.

Then, somehow, I can hear my dad whispering. He's praying to God for help. Even more surprising, I can hear my mom's voice too, begging Heavenly Father for deliverance. As they continue to repeat their pleas to God, my dad approaches the car. He's a small man, not known for incredible strength, but he begins to lift the car off of my beloved mother. A minute later, I continue to stand frozen in amazement as I see my mom, dad, and the three children standing at a safe distance from the car. They're perhaps bruised, but not broken. They've been saved through a miracle of God.

I learned a lot from this dream. One of the obvious lessons is that God answers our prayers, often through miraculous means. But even more striking to me is the love that I felt God had for my parents for willingly risking their lives to save the lives of others. That immensity of love is the same feeling I experience each time I'm in heaven, particularly when I see Jesus Christ. He and His Father are exceedingly pleased when we show godly love toward others—the kind of deep, abiding love that our Brother and Father show for all of us. And when we feel Their love, we'll want to share it with others even more.[1]

Visiting heaven has taught me so much about Christlike love—how to feel it myself and how to feel it for others. The love I've felt in heaven is so strong that it's permeated my heart and I can't help but share that love with others. It's a full, complete type of love that encompasses the feelings of safety, warmth, peace, joy, gratitude, and vibrancy. I want others to feel that complete, or perfect, love too. After all, that type of love is generous and selfless, not selfish.

Because I've experienced Christ's love, I'm also better able to see people as Christ and Heavenly Father do. Instead of defining people based on their weaknesses and what I don't like, now I see them as

unique sons and daughters of God. They have inherited divine quali-
ties from their heavenly parents and have the potential to live with
God in the eternities, just as I do.[2] If God sees the potential in His
children, then I certainly should too.

My first visit to heaven began a mighty change in my heart—a
change that continued as I had more dreams and felt more of Christ's
and God's love for me. At first, I thought my experiences in heaven
were the only cause of the change. But then I noticed that Richard was
experiencing his own change of heart. Surely, he was being influenced
by my heavenly excursions, but I knew there was more to it. And then
I realized: the most profound change began when we learned of The
Church of Jesus Christ of Latter-day Saints. The change continued
as we were baptized and then as we completed our ordinances in the
temple. And the change continues today.

Richard and I loved each other dearly before we began our journey toward an eternal marriage and an eternal family, but now we're
much better at showing our love for each other. We're much better at
behaving like we *want* to spend eternity together. Before, we would
push each other's buttons, saying things that weren't nice. We'd get
mad at each other. I would swear and throw things. Richard would
criticize. But not anymore. We see each other through new eyes and
with an eternal perspective. We know that our memories will last for
eternity, and we want to ensure they're uplifting memories filled with
love, not with frustration and pain. We're more affectionate now, and
we're much closer emotionally. As a result, we're also more in tune
with each other's needs.

With our increased love, we're also more patient with and forgiving of each other when we do slip up. We've learned to keep things
lighthearted. For example, Richard has the habit of leaving the cereal
box open, and in the past, I allowed myself to get worked up about
it. Silly, but true. To solve the problem, we decided to compromise:
we'd buy separate boxes of cereal—one for him, and one for me. If
he wants to keep his open, that's fine with me. Now instead of fighting about it, I can simply laugh. In other situations, we give a playful
reminder. For instance, if Richard forgets to put the toilet seat down,
I'll have him raise his hand and repeat after me: "I solemnly promise

to never do it again." Of course, if I expect him to keep that promise perfectly from here on out, I'm setting both of us up for grief. But if I can see that he's trying, then I feel appreciation for his efforts. That increases my love for him, and in return, he feels more love for me.[3]

Now that we don't argue like we used to, we have more time to discuss what really matters. We talk about religion, we set and discuss goals, and we talk about our family—those still living and those in heaven. We've learned that living this way has made marriage so rewarding. We feel so blessed that we not only will spend the rest of our mortal lives together but will also be inseparable in heaven for eternity.

Richard and I are also remarkably closer to family members who are still living. Before, weeks would go by without me talking to my parents, my sister, or my daughter. Now, I call them more often and tell them how much I love them. Both Richard and I are much more loving and accepting of our family members. My father and I have a long history of butting heads and getting into heated arguments. But now, I have no desire to be confrontational. I love my dad for who he is, and I try to understand him better. I remind myself that he's cranky because he's elderly and has difficulty moving around. I'm sure I'd tend to be cranky too!

Richard has stopped being critical of his brother and sister. Though both of them have very different priorities and beliefs than Richard, he's learned to accept and love his siblings rather than try to change them. He's working to strengthen his relationships with them, and he's also patient. I've similarly learned to be patient with my daughter, with whom I have a strained relationship. I hope that in time, she'll be ready to move above our past and know that we can be a family forever, but I won't push it. It doesn't do any good to try to force a square peg through a round hole. All you end up with is lots of dents in the peg and a bigger hole. If I have to wait until heaven, that's okay. With a gospel perspective, I realize that I don't have to fix everything. That's not my job; it's Heavenly Father's. If I do what I can, by always showing love for my daughter and by praying for her, then I've done my part. Heavenly Father will take care of the rest.

That perspective has brought Richard and me immense peace. We want all of our family members to experience the joy that has come to us through accepting Christ's gospel by being baptized into His church and going to the temple. However, so far only one relative—the wife of Richard's brother—has joined the Church. At first, our relatives' indifference toward the Church pained us. But we've learned to simply trust in God's plan. Either in mortality or in heaven, all of our family members will have the opportunity to learn about the gospel and then to accept it. We try to teach the gospel through how we live, and we clarify gospel principles when they come up, but we don't argue about religion with family members and we don't expect them to live by the principles we do. We don't look down on them or push them away because they're not keeping the commandments that Richard and I have been taught. We understand that we're most likely to bring people unto Christ when we exemplify Christlike love and extend it to them.[4]

Our love stretches beyond our family to everyone else we meet. I'm constantly aware that everyone I see is ultimately a brother or a sister because we all have the same Heavenly Father. I know that everyone on this earth is loved by hundreds and even thousands upon thousands of family members in heaven. It's like everyone's deceased ancestors are asking me to convey their love to their family here on earth. I feel compelled to show and share that love everywhere I go. When I'm in the movie theater, I feel love for everyone watching the film with me. When I'm in the grocery store, I feel like I know those in line with me and that I need to remind them that they're loved.

Numerous scriptures emphasize the need to love everyone around us—even those who treat us as enemies (see Luke 6:27, 35; John 14:15; 3 Nephi 12:44). Pure, Christlike love is called *charity* (see Moroni 7:47), and "except men shall have charity they cannot inherit that place which thou hast prepared in the mansions of thy Father" (Ether 12:34). The epitome of charity is Jesus's willingness to suffer and die for us. Though we aren't required to do the same, we are expected to bless others' lives by giving of ourselves—our talents, our time, and our means.[5]

Admittedly, developing charity isn't a task for one day. In fact, developing it requires us to "pray unto the Father with all the energy of heart" (Moroni 7:48)—it takes monumental effort! Charity is also a gift of the Spirit, meaning we can develop it with the help of the Holy Ghost if we are obedient.[6] Since we're not obedient 100 percent of the time, we'll also need to repent regularly if we want to develop Christlike love. To develop charity, we also need to practice. That practice involves serving others and making sacrifices to meet other people's needs and wants. Yes, we must go beyond meeting needs to meeting wants (see Mosiah 18:29). I believe that striving to fulfill people's wants, not just necessities, is a true indicator of charity. Charity also involves being tolerant of those around us, being patient when someone has fallen short, choosing not to be offended, and completely forgiving others. Further, we must accept others' weaknesses, look past physical appearance, and resist the urge to categorize.[7] To have charity, we must refuse to judge others. As President Thomas S. Monson explained, "There is really no way we can know the heart, the intentions, or the circumstances of someone who might say or do something we find reason to criticize. Thus the commandment: 'Judge not.'"[8] And as Mother Teresa declared, "If you judge people, you have no time to love them."[9]

Though charity may require great acts of service, sacrifice, and self-control (e.g., reining in the desire to lash out when someone is unkind to us), Christlike love also includes small acts of kindness. According to Dale Carnegie, we each have the "power to increase the sum total of this world's happiness . . . by giving a few words of sincere appreciation to someone who is lonely or discouraged. Perhaps you will forget tomorrow the kind words you say today, but the recipient may cherish them over a lifetime."[10] Similarly, Jeffrey R. Holland asserted that "pure Christlike love flowing from true righteousness can change the world."[11] I believe that to be true.

Our mighty change of heart isn't limited to how we view other people. Richard and I now have a totally different perspective on life. Richard used to be quite serious, and he'd get pretty upset when things went wrong or when other people were rude. His father was also serious, and maybe that's where Richard got it from. During one of my dreams, Junior told me that he regretted being so serious during mortality and that he didn't want Richard to make the same mistake. Junior's words helped Richard want to change, and the gospel of Jesus Christ gave him the power to transform. The change wasn't immediate, but the result has been dramatic. Now, when someone at work is rude, Richard shrugs it off. He'll find a reason to laugh about the situation, or he'll just let it go. He reminds himself that though his coworkers have different personalities, which sometimes clash, they're all God's children.

Taking offense and holding onto it hurts you, making you negative and bitter. Now, I don't know of anyone who aspires to be negative and bitter, but that's what so many people are unwittingly pursuing when they let themselves be angry and won't let go, as if it's a lifeline. In reality, it's a deathline, causing your heart to shrivel up. It's comparable to what smoking does to the lungs, causing them to turn black and preventing them from inflating fully—or even partly. Numerous organizations spend hundreds of millions of dollars to discourage people from smoking;[12] I'm of the opinion that a black, shriveled heart spiritually speaking is of even more concern. Just as it can be incredibly difficult to quit smoking, it can be an arduous task to open our hearts and decide not to hold on to anger. But there are noticeable immediate benefits when we stop either of these unhealthy habits. As just one example, within twenty minutes of not smoking, blood pressure and heart rate decrease.[13] The same happens when we decide not to take offense or be mad.[14] Another huge result is that life is so much more enjoyable. Richard is extraordinarily happier now because he's decided not to take situations so seriously or to become upset. I've learned to do the same. I used to have a fiery temper and would yell at others. Now, I don't get angry. I have no desire to. I'd much rather feel God's love for me and for others.

Richard has also stopped focusing on the negative. He tends to be an overachiever, and he would often get down on himself when he didn't meet his expectations, particularly regarding his work and earnings. He's learned to be happy with what he has. That's made my life particularly easier in one respect. I always had the hardest time picking out presents for him. Whatever I chose, Richard had something negative to say about it. One year, I arranged for him to have LASIK surgery. I thought I'd finally gotten something he'd like, but my hopes were dashed when I told him about the gift. "Why in the world did you get that for me?" he asked. Now, even if he doesn't love what I get him, he pretends to like it because he wants me to be happy. But also important, he doesn't focus on material possessions now, so he's more content with what we have and the small gifts I give him.

With these mighty changes of heart, Richard is much more like his mom. She has always focused on the positive. Each morning during her mortal life, she'd wake up in the morning and exclaim, "Oh my, it's a beautiful day! I can't wait to see what the day's going to bring."

Richard and I both focus on living our lives in a way that pleases Heavenly Father and Jesus Christ. Every day, we try to do something that will make our Savior smile. For Richard, it might be feeding our neighbor's horse. For me, it might be rescuing a kitten I find along the running trail, or it might be expressing my love for someone. I don't want to do or say anything that I'd be embarrassed about if Jesus were standing beside me. I want to be worthy of His companionship. When I am, I can feel Him smiling down on me. It's a blissful sensation of warmth—so much greater than what comes from the sun.

Another reason Richard and I are happier, more loving people is because we know of God's eternal plan for us and our family. Knowing that Heavenly Father has prepared a way for us to be with Him and our family for eternity has exponentially increased our gratitude. We also see how He's blessing us each moment of our lives; we know that happiness isn't reserved for heaven. We appreciate all that is around us—beautiful sunsets, our cats, friends, and trials that allow us to grow. I love to start the day by singing "How Great Thou Art," because I am truly awestruck by Heavenly Father's and Jesus Christ's goodness, majesty, love, mercy, and blessings. I'm grateful for songs that help me express my profound gratitude for this world we live in and all that God has provided—and will continue to provide—for me and everyone else.

With an eternal perspective, Richard and I are able to set aside our fears and worries. We know that God is in charge and will handle problems according to His timing. Nevertheless, I know it can be easy to become weighed down by even the small things. Recently, I was sitting in the temple and thinking about some problems that had come up that day. I was feeling a tad overwhelmed by those issues and the limited time I had to meet all my commitments. But then, through an interaction with another woman in the temple, the Spirit reminded me that most things that stress me out really aren't that important. In a week, or even a few hours, I'll have completely forgotten about them. So why should I let them bother me right now? I shouldn't. Instead, I should address them the best I can with Heavenly Father's help, and then I should move on.

Of course, that's not easy when we're faced with bigger challenges. But we can still keep our worrying in check if we maintain an eternal perspective. Neill F. Marriott explained that an eternal perspective is central to her family's motto "It will all work out." She wisely noted:

> Our family motto doesn't say, "It will all work out now." It speaks of our hope in the eternal outcome—not necessarily of present results. Scripture says, "Search diligently, pray always, and be believing, and all things shall work together for your good." This doesn't mean all things are good, but for the meek and faithful, things—both positive and negative—work together for good, and the timing is the Lord's. We wait on Him, sometimes like Job in his suffering, knowing that God "maketh sore, and bindeth up: he woundeth, and his hands make whole." A meek heart accepts the trial and the waiting for that time of healing and wholeness to come.[15]

If we have faith and keep the commandments, we don't need to fear. In fact, when we have faith and confidence in our standing before God, there's no room for fear.[16] That's why the Lord has told us to "look unto me in every thought; doubt not, fear not" (D&C 6:36). If we constantly focus on Christ and Heavenly Father, we remember that They are aware of us and will come to our aid. As we're reminded in Isaiah 41:10, "Fear thou not; for I am with thee: be not dismayed; for I am thy God: I will strengthen thee; yea, I will help thee; yea, I will uphold thee with the right hand of my righteousness."[17] Richard and I have taken to heart the counsel in Matthew 6. Verses 28–29 tell us to "consider the lilies of the field, how they grow; they toil not, neither do they spin: And yet I say unto you, That even Solomon in all his glory was not arrayed like one of these." Later in the chapter, we're promised that God knows all things that we are in need of and that if we seek "first the kingdom of God, and his righteousness," all needful "things shall be added unto" us (Matthew 6:32–33).

Trusting in God has also enabled us to accept and bear our trials with patience—and even cheerfulness.[18] We can, as Joseph B. Wirthlin counseled, let "come what may, and love it." With this attitude, "our hardest times can be times of greatest growth, which in turn can lead toward times of greatest happiness."[19] I absolutely love what Linda S. Reeves has said about enduring hard times: "I do not know why we have the many trials that we have, but it is my personal feeling that the reward is so great, so eternal and everlasting, so joyful and beyond our understanding that in that day of reward, we may feel to say to our merciful, loving Father, 'Was that *all* that was required?'" This is the perspective we need to maintain. Even if our trials seemingly bring us to the breaking point, hold on! What is in store for us is worth anything that we may experience in mortality. So, when your trials make you fall to your knees, be grateful: "What will it matter," Sister Reeves asks, "what we suffered here if, in the end, those trials are the very things which qualify us for eternal life and exaltation in the kingdom of God with our Father and Savior?" Don't ever give up, and don't ever lose hope or faith. Remember, look for, and draw upon the deep, abiding love that Heavenly Father and the Savior have for you. Knowing that you can be encompassed in their love eternally will help you do what's needed here so you can return to them in heaven.[20]

We can even declare, "Come what may," when family members die. We know that our separation from them is temporary. We will be united again, in a world far more amazing than this imperfect one. True, that knowledge doesn't take away all pain, but it does provide comfort. This past year, my mother passed away. At times I've felt crushing sorrow, but overall, I'm so grateful that she was released from this life. She had been in overwhelming pain prior to dying, and now she's free. I know she's at peace now, and I rejoice for her. She's surrounded by her ancestors, engulfed in their love, and she has the opportunity to learn about Christ's true gospel. My heart swells with gratitude because I know that my mom is okay. I can patiently wait until it's my time to join her.

The mighty change of heart that Richard and I have experienced has affected every part of our lives—in so many more ways than I can describe here. We're certainly better people today than we were ten years ago, before I learned what heaven is all about and before we started our journey to God's true Church. We're new people, and the transformation has been thrilling. But we're not perfect, and we know that every day we need to change a little more, bit by bit becoming more like Christ, our perfect example (see 3 Nephi 12:48).

NOTES

1. Joseph Smith taught that "love is one of the chief characteristics of Deity, and ou[gh]t to be manifested by those who aspire to be the sons of God. A man filled with the love of God, is not content with blessing his family alone, but ranges through the whole world, anxious to bless the whole human race" (Letter to the Council of the Twelve, December 15, 1840, http://josephsmithpapers.org/paperSummary /letter-to-the-council-of-the-twelve-15-december-1840).

2. I agree with Rosemary M. Wixom's assertion that "once we begin to see the divinity in ourselves, we can see it in others" ("Discovering the Divinity Within," *Ensign*, November 2015).

3. In this respect (as in all other areas), we need to follow our Father's example. "He rejoices every time we take a step forward. To Him, our direction is ever more important than our speed" (Larry R. Lawrence, "What Lack I Yet," *Ensign*, November 2015).

4. Susan W. Tanner, "'I Am the Light Which Ye Shall Hold Up,'" *Ensign*, May 2006.

5. Robert J. Whetten, "True Followers," *Ensign*, May 1999.

6. Whetten, "True Followers."

7. See Thomas S. Monson, "Charity Never Faileth," *Ensign*, November 2010.

8. Monson, "Charity Never Faileth."

9. Mother Teresa, in R. M. Lala, *A Touch of Greatness: Encounters with the Eminent* (New York: Penguin, 2001), x.

10. Dale Carnegie, in Dakota Livesay, *Living the Code: Seven Principles That Could Change Your Life* (Bloomington, IN: Xlibris, 2013), 176.

11. Jeffrey R. Holland, "The Cost and Blessings of Discipleship," *Ensign*, May 2014.

12. It was projected that in the United States alone, state governments would spend $721.6 million in 2018 on such programs ("Fast Facts," Centers for Disease Control and Prevention, accessed March 2, 2018, http://www.cdc.gov/tobacco/data_statistics/fact_sheets/fast_facts).

13. "Smoke-Free Living: Benefits and Milestones," American Heart Association, June 11, 2015, http://www.heart.org/HEARTORG/GettingHealthy/QuitSmoking/YourNon-SmokingLife/Smoke-free-Living-Benefits-Milestones_UCM_322711_Article.jsp#.Vlo7Z3arT4Y.

14. LaVelle Hendricks, Sam Bore, Dean Aslinia, and Guy Morriss, "The Effects of Anger on the Brain and Body," *National Forum Journal of Counseling and Addiction* 2, no. 1 (2013): 1–12.

15. Neill F. Marriott, "Yielding Our Hearts to God," *Ensign*, November 2015. This understanding helped her family heal after Neill's twenty-one-year-old daughter died from a bicycle accident. I encourage you to read the entire article for guidance on achieving a mighty change of heart.

16. See David A. Bednar, "Therefore They Hushed Their Fears," *Ensign*, May 2015.

17. Doctrine and Covenants 68:6 tells us that because Jesus Christ stands beside us, in addition to not fearing, we should be cheerful.

18. For another example of enduring trials patiently and cheerfully, see Mosiah 24:12–16. It truly is possible.

19. Elder Wirthlin received the counsel to let "come what may, and love it" from his mother after his football team was defeated in a tough game. Over the ensuing years, he learned that we can take specific steps to embrace his mother's counsel. These steps include learning to laugh, particularly at ourselves; keeping an eternal perspective; recognizing that Heavenly Father will compensate us for every loss we experience, if we are faithful; and trusting that Heavenly Father and Jesus will give us the strength to bear our burdens ("Come What May, and Love It," *Ensign*, November 2008).

20. Linda S. Reeves, "Worthy of Our Promised Blessings," *Ensign*, November 2015.

Chapter 10

Let Your Light So Shine

A tall, handsome young man is talking with an older man and woman who are holding hands. The young man's eyes are shining, and as his words float my way, I understand why he looks so happy. He's sharing the good news of Christ's gospel.

He looks familiar, and I wonder whether he's a relative. As the possibilities run through my mind, suddenly I gasp. I haven't actually met him before, but I know who he is. He's not a relative—not by blood, anyway—but I feel a kinship with him. He's the son of a member of my church family, and I recently grieved with his mother when he was hit by a car while serving a proselytizing mission in Sweden. Elder Mason Bailey was a pure young man, willing to devote two years of his life to the Lord by sharing the gospel message with all who would listen. But his time had been cut heartbreakingly short. Some people might ask how a loving Heavenly Father could allow a righteous missionary's life to be taken. After all, he was engaged in the most important work on the earth.

As I watch him teaching the gospel in heaven, I realize that he's still engaged in God's most important work. The only real difference is where he's doing it. I feel peace as I see how content he is. I'm sure he misses his family members who are still on earth, but I know that he's surrounded by family in heaven and that he feels the joy of helping individuals prepare to accept Christ's gospel (see D&C 18:15–16).

As I continue to watch him with this older couple, and later as I see him teaching others in heaven how to be missionaries, it's clear that every word he speaks, every gesture, is based on love—love for Heavenly Father, for our Savior, and for those he's interacting with. I'm excited to return to earth and tell Mason's mother what I've seen. I want her to understand what I now understand—that her precious Mason is okay, that he has a purpose and is still serving God. She has every reason to continue being proud of her son. And she can have confidence that if she remains faithful, she'll spend eternity with him. While the loss of her son may still be painful, she can be filled with hope and gratitude for God's merciful plan of eternal families.

Whether in mortality or in heaven, sharing the gospel is the most important work we can be involved in.[1] That's because it's not our work but God's work—and His glory. His greatest desire, the objective of all He does, is to "bring to pass the immortality and eternal life of man" (Moses 1:39). I have received multiple witnesses that sharing the gospel is essential. Dream after dream, those in heaven have told me that they want their families on earth to learn about the restored gospel. The reason is twofold: First, they want their family members to experience the joy of the gospel while living. I can testify from personal experience that life on earth is so much better through learning of God's plan, being baptized into His Church, and keeping His commandments. Second, they want their family members to learn about the gospel so that the family members will eventually complete temple ordinances for deceased ancestors. These deceased family members are eager to have their temple work completed so that they can progress in heaven and so that they can be sealed to their family members for eternity.

These angels, these family members in heaven, are the reason I felt compelled to write this book. They've repeatedly implored me, "Please, tell my family. Tell them your story so they might understand God's great work. His gospel is the most important thing they can ever learn about during life. And their learning about it is the most important thing for us too." I've felt overwhelmed with this task of sharing what I've learned. I'm not a writer. I feel like Moroni when he prayed to the Lord, saying: "Thou hast not made us [the authors of the Book of Mormon] mighty in writing. . . . When we write we behold our weakness, and stumble because of the placing of our words" (Ether 12:24–25). But Heavenly Father has asked me to write this book, and I know that He provides assistance when we try our best to obey Him. I certainly have felt His help as I've worked on this book. Insights have come to me that I know came through the Holy Ghost, not my own understanding. I know that just as I've been guided in what to write, God will continue to assist with the book, helping get it into the hands of those who are ready to learn more about Him, His doctrine, and His Church.

Though writing this book has felt daunting at times, sharing God's message of love is a different story. I could talk day and night about my visits to heaven, my experience finding Christ's true church, and how amazing my life is as a member of The Church of Jesus Christ of Latter-day Saints. My knowledge of Jesus Christ's love for everyone and the opportunity to live with our families forever excites me so much that I can barely restrain myself from telling everyone about these truths. This world can be immensely confusing and filled with conflict. It's difficult to know where to turn for direction and how to find happiness. Christ's Church answers life's most important questions. His Church has done that for me, even answering questions I didn't realize I had. His gospel is complete, and it completes us. I'm happier every day of my life because of the relationship I've developed with the Savior and Heavenly Father, and I want everyone to obtain that same happiness.

That desire is the same reason 74,079 men and women chose to serve proselytizing missions for the Church in 2015.[2] Their desire is to share God's love with everyone and to teach of God's great plan for His children.[3] I love the missionaries for this desire and their willingness to sacrifice eighteen, twenty-four, or more months of their lives to share God's message with others. I also love the missionaries because they helped Richard and me on our journey to becoming members of Christ's true church. They taught us the foundational principles of the gospel—all of which align with what I learned in heaven. They taught us how to pray and how to keep God's commandments. Then they baptized us and conferred upon us the gift of the Holy Ghost, following the pattern established anciently (see Acts 8:12, 15).

The two missionaries who taught Richard and me the gospel will always have a special place in my heart. Once, when I was sharing a lesson about missionaries with children in my local congregation, I said that missionaries are my BFFs (best friends forever).[4]

And I believe that's truly the case. The two missionaries who were instrumental in my conversion will be my very dear friends for eternity. I'll always be grateful for them, and I believe I'll continue to talk with them in heaven.

Just as the missionaries have a purpose—to preach the gospel and bring others unto Christ—I also have a purpose. Like the missionaries, I've been called to tell young and old about Christ's church and forever families, and to help others complete essential gospel ordinances. This is the calling Heavenly Father has given me. It's my purpose, and it's Richard's purpose. We're amazingly grateful to know what our purpose in life is. Before, Richard and I lacked direction. Our lives had little meaning because we didn't know there was more to life than simply muddling through and seeking fleeting fulfillment. All that has changed, and now I want others to realize that their lives also have purpose. Our grand purpose is to return to God, having qualified to dwell with Him and our families eternally in the celestial kingdom. As we work toward fulfilling that purpose, we are also called on to help others fulfill that purpose for themselves.

The call to preach Christ's gospel isn't new. Many prophets were commissioned during Old Testament times to declare God's word to all inhabitants of the earth.[5] John the Baptist prepared the way for Jesus Christ's ministry, and then He appointed twelve apostles to teach His doctrine. After He died and was resurrected, He once again appeared to the Apostles and gave the following directive: "Go ye therefore, and teach all nations, baptizing them in the name of the Father, and of the Son, and of the Holy Ghost: Teaching them to observe all things whatsoever I have commanded you" (Matthew 28:19–20; see also Mark 15:16). That mandate is no less important today than it was during Christ's ministry two millennia ago. President Dallin H. Oaks has explained that "proclaim[ing] the good news of the gospel of Jesus Christ is a fundamental principle of the Christian faith."[6]

In fact, members of The Church of Jesus Christ of Latter-day Saints promise as part of the baptismal covenant that they'll share the gospel. Those who enter Christ's Church promise "to stand as witnesses of God at all times and in all things, and in all places that [they] may be in, even until death" (Mosiah 18:9). As Church members go to the temple and complete additional ordinances, they pledge to serve God with "heart, might, mind and strength" (D&C 4:2). I believe that the greatest service we can give to Heavenly Father is to help Him fulfill His work and glory of bringing to pass the "immortality and eternal life" of His children (Moses 1:39).[7]

Interestingly, John A. Widtsoe, an Apostle from 1921 to 1952, said that our promise to teach the gospel started even before we arrived on the earth. He said that while in the premortal life in heaven, "We agreed, right then and there, to be not only saviors for ourselves but . . . saviors for the whole human family. We went into a partnership with the Lord. The working out of the plan became then not merely the Father's work, and the Savior's work, but also our work. The least of us, the humblest, is in partnership with the Almighty in achieving the purpose of the eternal plan of salvation."[8]

Even with a knowledge that we've promised to teach Christ's gospel to others, many people aren't engaged in the work. Perhaps they're not sure how to, they're shy, or they think they're too busy. I realize that each of these reasons is a legitimate barrier to being a missionary,[9] but we can overcome them, particularly if we ask for God's help. Also,

1 John 4:18 says, "perfect love"—of God, of the gospel, and of all people—"casteth out fear."

We need to become excited about sharing the gospel. We can develop enthusiasm by strengthening our relationship with the Savior. David A. Bednar explained that "devoted disciples of Jesus Christ always have been and always will be valiant missionaries."[10] With a strong relationship with Jesus, we'll recognize how valuable the gospel is. And when we've found something of extraordinary value, don't we want to share it with others? We can see that in the story of the woman who met Jesus at a well in Samaria. After talking with Him, she was convinced He was the promised Messiah. What was her reaction? She immediately wanted to tell everyone she knew. She was so excited that she left her water container by the well and went into the city, likely at a run. Upon arriving, she urged others to "come, see a man, which told me all things that ever I did: is not this the Christ?" (John 4:29).

As another example, let's consider a parable of sorts that Elder Bednar shared. Years ago, he and his wife watched as two of their young sons played outside. One of the Bednars' sons became slightly injured, and the parents decided to see how the boys would react. The older, uninjured boy led his brother into the house and then proceeded to clean the scratched arm. After drying off his brother's arm, the older boy applied almost an entire tube of ointment, followed by bandages from elbow to wrist, even though the scratch was small. With the injury cared for, both boys had smiles on their faces. The little brother gathered up the ointment and more bandages, then headed outside. He approached his friends and then enthusiastically put ointment and bandages on them.

After recounting this story, Elder Bednar said: "Why did that little boy do what he did? Please note that he immediately and intuitively wanted to give to his friends the very thing that had helped him when he was hurt. That little boy did not have to be urged, challenged, prompted, or goaded to act. His desire to share was the natural consequence of a most helpful and beneficial personal experience." When we experience the glorious healing, cleansing, renewing, and comforting results of the gospel in our lives, we too want to share this "medicine" with others. Elder Bednar admitted that in our eagerness to tell others about this healing balm, "We may be awkward or abrupt or even relentless in our attempts." But "our simple desire is to share . . . the truths that are of greatest worth to us."[11]

So how do we heed the mandate to share the gospel with others, aside from serving a full-time proselytizing mission? We can start by living the gospel to best of our abilities. Jeffrey R. Holland noted, "Surely there is no more powerful missionary message we can send to this world than the example of a loving and happy Latter-day Saint life. The manner and bearing, the smile and kindness of a faithful member of the Church brings a warmth and an outreach which no missionary tract or videotape can convey."[12]

We should also pray—pray that we will have opportunities to share what we know, that we will know what to say when the moment arrives, and that others will have soft hearts and be prepared to accept our message. As we're reminded in Doctrine and Covenants 123:12, "There are many yet on the earth . . . who are only kept from the truth because they know not where to find it." We need to pray that they will find us![13] Neil L. Andersen emphasized that missionary work is a partnership between us and God: "Our desire to share the gospel takes all of us to our knees, and it should, because we need the Lord's help." Elder Andersen then gave this powerful promise: "As you pray to know with whom to speak, names and faces will come into your mind. Words to speak will be given in the very moment you need them. Opportunities will open to you. . . . The Lord will bless you with your very own miracles." Our Heavenly Father, who wants all to hear and embrace the gospel, will answer our prayers by opening doors and removing roadblocks.[14]

Just as important, we should pray to feel God's love for those who have not yet been introduced to or embraced the truth.[15] To truly love them and serve them by teaching them Christ's doctrine, we must view them through the eyes of a parent—not just any parent but our wise, compassionate Heavenly Father, He who sees each child's true worth and divine potential.[16]

Another preparatory step we need to take is to follow Peter's counsel to "be ready always to give an answer to every man that asketh you a reason of the hope that is in you" (1 Peter 3:15). That instruction makes sense to me, but it's still a little abstract. What are concrete ways to be ready? I think a lot of our preparation involves studying the scriptures so we have a knowledge base to draw upon. If we've regularly and earnestly studied the scriptures, the Holy Ghost will help bring to mind the verses that will be the most effective to share with a specific person (see John 14:26; D&C 14:8; 100:5–6, 8). We should also read Church magazines so we're familiar with what Heavenly Father is telling us through our prophets and other Church leaders. In addition, it will be helpful if we're familiar with (and, even better, if we've memorized) the thirteen Articles of Faith, "The Living Christ," and "The Family: A Proclamation to the World." Each of these resources contains a concise presentation of fundamental doctrines in Christ's true Church.

We can also facilitate gospel discussions by not shying away from mentioning our involvement in Church activities and spiritual experiences. As an example, when a coworker or classmate asks about our weekend, we can say, "On Sunday, I taught a Sunday School lesson on XYZ. The class members shared some great insights." Or perhaps, "I went to my church's temple on Saturday, and it was so great—my stress melted away." Such comments will likely pique the interest of others, and they might ask you for more details. That's a great time to invite them to learn more—or even to join you next week at church, a Church event, or simply a casual activity with your family.

Sure, they might not be ready for an invitation to meet with the missionaries, but that's okay. Simply sharing ways in which the gospel is part of your life—and makes you a happier, better person—is a way to let your light shine. Others will recognize that light and may eventually desire to have that light in their own lives. Remember, our role is to share the gospel, not to convince others to believe what we're saying and decide to join Christ's Church. That decision is a very personal one and can only be made by that individual.[17] Even if someone isn't interested, that doesn't mean we've failed. In fact, it's impossible to fail when we've tried our best to share the gospel.[18] And, of course, when someone chooses not to accept our invitation, we should still respect them, love them, and be their friend. Neil L. Andersen assured that regardless of how a person responds to an invitation, "You will feel the approval of the Lord and, with that approval, an added measure of faith to share your beliefs again and again."[19]

And now a few words for those who are on the receiving end of this message about Christ. Just as I will continue to respect and love you even if you aren't interested in my message, I hope you'll continue to respect me for wanting to share what I believe to be a marvelous message. In fact, try to see it as a compliment. I care enough about you that I want you to experience the same joy that I've been blessed with since learning about Christ's gospel. I'm in no way trying to coerce you to accept what I believe. Rather, I'm extending to you an invitation to learn more, to pray, and to try out Christ's teachings for yourself.[20] It's essential for you to learn for yourself that Christ's Church has been restored to the earth and that through it, you can live eternally with your family in God's presence.[21]

Please also recognize that when I invite you to learn more about the Savior and The Church of Jesus Christ of Latter-day Saints, I'm not implying that you're a sinful person or a heathen. And I'm not trying to discredit your current religious traditions.[22] I encourage you to hold on to everything you know to be true and praiseworthy—and to make room for the message I'm sharing. The Savior entreated His disciples to "come and see" (John 1:39). I likewise urge you to come and see—test it out. See for yourself whether Christ's gospel has been restored in The Church of Jesus Christ of Latter-day Saints and how it enriches and expands upon your current beliefs.[23]

Each day, I pray that you and every other child of God—that's everyone!—will find the peace, love, and happiness that I've found through my dreams and through joining Christ's Church. I pray that you will come to know that you can be reunited with loved ones, God, and Jesus Christ. I pray that you will accept Christ as your personal Savior and that you will choose to be baptized so that you can become clean and eventually "enter into the kingdom of God" (John 3:5). If you could see what I've seen in heaven, you would believe as I do. But you don't need visions of heaven to know for yourself. Our loving Heavenly Father will reveal the truth to you if you'll but desire to believe. Nurture that desire by studying God's word in the Bible. Then examine how the Book of Mormon, Doctrine and Covenants, and Pearl of Great Price clarify and add to your understanding of God's plan, particularly the role of Jesus Christ. He truly lived a sinless life, which enabled Him to atone for our sins. Nowhere is his role described more clearly than in Alma 7:11–13:

> And he shall go forth, suffering pains and afflictions and temptations of every kind; and this that the word might be fulfilled which saith he will take upon him the pains and the sicknesses of his people.
>
> And he will take upon him death, that he may loose the bands of death which bind his people; and he will take upon him their infirmities, that his bowels may be filled with mercy, according to the flesh, that he may know according to the flesh how to succor his people according to their infirmities.
>
> Now the Spirit knoweth all things; nevertheless the Son of God suffereth according to the flesh that he might take upon him the sins of his people, that he might blot out their transgressions according to the power of his deliverance; and now behold, this is the testimony which is in me.

He willingly gave His life so that we could be forgiven of our sins and become more like Him. But He did even more than that. He suffered for our every pain—even those unrelated to sin. That act of love astounds me. I'm humbled that He was willing to endure every pain I—and you—will ever experience because He wanted to know how to succor us, to come to our aid and wipe away our tears. He did it because He wants us to be happy, now as well as in eternity. And I truly am happy because of this knowledge and everything else that I've learned and experienced through His gospel, which He restored to the earth through Joseph Smith. You can experience this same happiness—this joy—for yourself. Come and see. He is patiently waiting for you with outstretched arms, ready to embrace you (see 2 Nephi 1:15; Alma 5:33).

Even if you haven't been much of a missionary in the past—and even if the thought brings fear to your heart—now is the time to let your light shine, to share the joyful message of Christ's reality; God's love for each of His children; and the gospel's path to living with our Savior, our Heavenly Father, and our family for eternity. I am truly inspired by Elder Neil L. Andersen's appeal: "If you're not a full-time missionary with a missionary badge pinned on your coat, now is the time to paint one on your heart—painted, as Paul said, 'not with ink, but with the Spirit of the living God.'"[24]

God and Jesus Christ are counting on us—and so are our deceased family members and billions still on the earth. Our Father in Heaven will give us the strength to be missionaries—to paint a missionary badge on our hearts. He has given me the strength to do things I didn't want to do. And with His help, those experiences have been so rewarding. I've felt His overwhelming love for me and His approval that I did what He desired. I know the same will happen for you if you will help Him in His work. As you move forward, you won't be walking alone. You'll be accompanied by angels, just as I have been.[25] Because they want their family members to learn about and accept the gospel, these angels will assist you in your efforts to be missionaries.

Through engaging in the work, we also feel Heavenly Father and Jesus Christ smiling down on us. When I'm sharing the gospel message with others, I feel a blanket of love enfold me—God's love for me, His love for the person I'm talking with, and my own increased love for that person. Recently, I had the beautiful opportunity to accompany someone on her own journey of coming unto Christ. I sat with her as two full-time missionaries for The Church of Jesus Christ of Latter-day Saints taught her about God's plan of salvation—His plan for her! I testified that the missionaries' words were true. As I joined in these lessons, I learned more myself and gained new insights. I drew closer to the Lord through this experience, and I know the same will be true for you as you join in missionary work.

I've noticed an additional blessing that comes from sharing the gospel. When you're preaching the gospel, and therefore feeling greater love and coming unto Christ, life is happier. Bad news isn't as distressing. You're less likely to become irritated with people or with plans that go awry. You feel full, regardless of what comes your way. That's what happens when you're on the Lord's errand.

I will never stop being a missionary, not even after I leave this mortal life. I won't be deterred, even if others don't accept Christ's message. Proclaiming His word is my purpose, and I will fulfill it. Please join with me, join with God in achieving His grand purpose of "bring[ing] to pass the immortality and eternal life of man." That is how we will one day be united with our families for eternity, never to be separated. That is His plan. That is what I've learned through my glorious visions of heaven.

NOTES

1. See *Teachings of the Prophet Joseph Smith*, sel. Joseph Fielding Smith (Salt Lake City, UT: The Church of Jesus Christ of Latter-day Saints, 1976), 113.
2. "Statistical Report, 2015," *Church News*, April 2, 2016, https://www.lds.org/church/news/april-2015-general-conference-news-and-announcements.
3. This plan goes by many names, including the plan of happiness and the plan of salvation, and encompasses Christ's gospel. The purpose of the plan is to achieve God's work and glory: "To bring to pass the immortality and eternal life of man" (Moses 1:39).
4. As a side note, I hadn't planned to mention BFFs during the lesson. In fact, I didn't even know what *BFF* meant! What I'd been planning to say completely left my mind and was replaced by what the Holy Ghost wanted me to say. He knew what a BFF is, and He knew the children would understand. I could tell that they did by the shine in

their eyes and their wide smiles. It was obvious that the Holy Ghost's words helped these children feel a stronger love for the missionaries and also desire to share Christ's message of good news with others.

5. Just a few examples include Noah, Joshua, Isaiah, Jeremiah, and Jonah.

6. Dallin H. Oaks, "Sharing the Gospel," *Ensign,* November 2001.

7. Carol F. McConkie likewise suggested that Doctrine and Covenants 4:2 refers to putting our everything into the work of salvation, which includes missionary work, family history and temple work, and gospel instruction ("Here to Serve a Righteous Cause," *Ensign,* November 2015).

8. John A. Widtsoe, "The Worth of Souls," *Utah Genealogical and Historical Magazine,* October 1934, 189.

9. While we may think of a missionary as someone who devotes his or her life, at least for a time, to preaching the gospel, the definition isn't that narrow; everyone can be a missionary. Elder Bednar said that "a missionary is a follower of Christ who testifies of Him as the Redeemer and proclaims the truths of His gospel" ("Come and See," *Ensign,* November 2014).

10. Bednar, "Come and See."

11. Bednar, "Come and See."

12. Jeffrey R. Holland, "Witnesses unto Me," *Ensign,* May 2001.

13. Holland, "Witnesses unto Me."

14. Neil L. Andersen, "It's a Miracle," *Ensign,* May 2013.

15. Dallin H. Oaks said, "The most effective missionaries, member and full-time, always act out of love" ("Sharing the Gospel").

16. See Dale G. Renlund, "Through God's Eyes," *Ensign,* November 2015, and Dieter F. Uchtdorf, "It Works Wonderfully," *Ensign,* November 2015.

17. Dallin H. Oaks explained, "The Lord loves all of His children. He desires that all have the fulness of His truth and the abundance of His blessings. He knows when they are ready, and He wants us to hear and heed His directions on sharing His gospel. When we do so, those who are prepared will respond to the message" ("Sharing the Gospel"). Neil L. Andersen added, "As surely as the Lord has inspired more missionaries to serve, He is also awakening the minds and opening the hearts of more good and honest people to receive His missionaries. You already know them or will know them. They are in your family and live in your neighborhood. They walk past you on the street, sit by you in school, and connect with you online" ("It's a Miracle").

18. See M. Russell Ballard, "Put Your Trust in the Lord," *Ensign,* November 2013.

19. Andersen, "It's a Miracle."

20. Bednar, "Come and See."

21. To gain your own witness that Christ's gospel is found in The Church of Jesus Christ of Latter-day Saints, follow the process outlined in Moroni 10:4–5. You must ask God in prayer, with faith and a true desire to receive an answer from Him. If you do these things, Christ "will manifest the truth of it unto you, by the power of the Holy Ghost" (vs. 4).

22. See Bednar, "Come and See."

23. See Bednar, "Come and See."

24. Andersen, "It's a Miracle."

25. "We join with faithful sisters [and brothers] of the past . . . when we join together in the work of salvation!" (Carol F. McConkie, "Here to Serve a Righteous Cause").

Acknowledgments

I would like to thank Suzy Bills for holding my hand through this process and for everything else she has given me: love, support, knowledge, friendship, an awesome insight from an LDS sister who was born into the Covenant, and most of all, this book. I would also like to thank Aaron Whelan and Kadan McMurtrey, my LDS missionaries who taught me scriptures, eternity, and a love for Heavenly Father and Jesus Christ beyond comparison. I am honored and humbled to be a part of your lives.

About the Author

JANE MOE

Jane Moe currently lives in Provo with her husband, Richard. In 2006, Jane survived a near-death experience. Her husband was waiting for her in recovery, and although groggy from the anesthesia, Jane was able to share with him the miracle she had just experienced. The veil between heaven and earth was gone and Jane became fascinated about what happens when we die. Her previous book, *What Heaven Is Like*, is released under her maiden name, Jane Lea Dykstra.

Scan to visit

www.janemoe.com

About the Author

SUZY BILLS

S uzy Bills is an assistant teaching professor of editing at Brigham Young University. She also owns a writing and editing business and was previously a lead editor at the Joseph Smith Papers Project. She loves sharing her skills with others, whether through teaching, mentoring, helping people get their thoughts and experiences on paper, or fine-tuning their writing. When she's not teaching, writing, or editing, she's probably training for her next marathon.

Working on *Visions of Heaven* was a gift for Suzy. She was fascinated to hear about Jane's dreams, and as Jane described the love she felt from deceased family members and from Jesus Christ, Suzy felt that same love. Through hearing Jane's experiences and doing research for this book, Suzy gained additional insights about heaven and the gospel principles that will allow her to live eternally with her family. In this book, Suzy shares some of her personal insights and relevant experiences as she discusses gospel principles in connection with Jane's dreams.